Steve,

   May this be a handy
tool as you share your
Unconditional Joy with
others.

Unconditional

Joy

Glenn W. Newell

426-1193

HOW TO GET IT, HAVE IT, AND KEEP IT

Unconditional Joy

HOW TO GET IT, HAVE IT, AND KEEP IT

DR. GLENN W. NOWELL

W

WHITAKER
HOUSE

UNCONDITIONAL JOY

Dr. Glenn W. Nowell
Hillview Baptist Church
5319 Dixie Highway
Louisville, KT 40216

ISBN: 0-88368-713-5
Printed in the United States of America
© 2001 by Glenn W. Nowell

Whitaker House
30 Hunt Valley Circle
New Kensington, PA 15068

Library of Congress Cataloging-in-Publication Data

Nowell, Glenn W., 1952–
  Unconditional joy: how to get it, have it, and keep it / Glenn W. Nowell.
      p. cm.
  ISBN 0-88368-713-5 (pbk. : alk. paper)
    1. Spiritual life. I. Title.
  BV4501.3 .N68 2001
  248.4—dc21

                                2001005369

1 2 3 4 5 6 7 8 9 10 11 12 / 09 08 07 06 05 04 03 02 01

Contents

Dedication

TO MY FAMILY

Acknowledgments

I cannot rave enough about the pure, often serene joy of an intensely intimate personal relationship with God. God has used many people in my life to nurture this spiritual consciousness to fruition, and to each individual I am deeply grateful. I would like to express my indebtedness to Mr. Bill Wilson and Dr. Bob Smith, cofounders of Alcoholics Anonymous, to the men and women of AA, and to countless dedicated members of other twelve-step organizations for restoring a truly holistic approach to healing and wellness. Much of the wisdom in this project has been lifted almost verbatim from discussions with many of these people and from a study of their literature.

I am especially indebted to my father, George W. Nowell, who has throughout my life inspired me by demonstrating the application of spiritual principles in his own life. Catherine McLemore Nowell, my mother, has endowed me with the advantage of deep maternal devotion. My wife, Michaela, has supported this project as a friend, sweetheart, constructive critic, and proofreader par excellence. Wes Nowell, my teenage son, has routinely amazed me with divinely-inspired insight, and he is living proof that spiritual principles can be courageously practiced at any age.

I appreciate the initiatives of Mr. Joe Paul Pruett in setting me on the initial track toward the publication of this manuscript. Dr. Bill Mackey, Executive Director of the Kentucky Baptist Convention; Dr. Jon Johnston, Professor of Sociology, Pepperdine University; and the Rev. Rusty Russell, Minister, Southeast Christian Church, Louisville,

Kentucky, in their own inspiring and supportive ways helped bring this project to fruition. Lifelong friend, the Rev. Jim Cavender, Jr., provided critical insight into this project, as did my friend in scholarship, Dr. Randy Webber. Mr. Jim Rill of Whitaker House saw value in my rough manuscript, and editor Jodi Henkiel turned it into a delightfully polished package.

Finally, I would like to thank the members of Hillview Baptist Church (HBC), Louisville, Kentucky, for their support and encouragement. The contributions of deacons Barry Caudill and Logan Ott were particularly helpful. Phyllis Mitchell, HBC's Minister of Administration, meticulously typed and proofed these pages with enthusiasm and encouragement. She contributed immensely to this undertaking. Buddy Bradshaw, John Posch, Dennis and Doris Jones, and David McNair introduced me to this wonderful way of living by serving as confidants, mentors, and soul mates. The contributions of and the gratitude for each of the individuals mentioned in the above paragraphs cannot be overstated.

The Must-read Preface

You've heard of unconditional love. How would you like to have *unconditional joy?* That's right, joy no matter what—joy amid the rotten frustrations that aggravate us throughout the day—joy even in the face of illness, tragedy, or impending doom. Yes, *unconditional joy.* The following pages tell you how to get it, have it, and keep it! This is not some wild scheme to get you to buy this book, and you will not be asked to accept the tenets of some weird religion or philosophy. The spirituality advocated here in no way steps outside the boundaries of biblical Christianity.

True biblical spirituality is all about your relationships, with God first and then with your fellow human beings. (See Matthew 22:37–39.) When you do your part to nurture these relationships, unconditional joy is a guaranteed result. (See Matthew 5:3–10.)

For many, spirituality has a mysterious connotation. What do you think of when you hear or use the word? For some, the psychic hot line comes to mind. For others, spiritual people are those who cloister or isolate themselves in order to dedicate themselves to God. Still others consider a spiritual person to be one who possesses a divine gift, such as the ability to heal. Spirituality may very well involve cloistering, and God does endow His people with spiritual gifts. However, in the case of the fortune-teller, the isolationist, and the glory seeker, they are polar opposites of the biblical description of spirituality.

True spirituality is a matter of letting go and allowing God to do for you what you cannot do for yourself. It is the process of emptying yourself of your swollen, deformed ego and allowing God to fill your emptiness as only He can. *Unconditional Joy: How to Get It, Have It, and Keep It* introduces you to seven simple action steps contained in the Beatitudes (Matt. 5:3–10) and explained as *The Promises*, beginning on page 16. Here is the bottom line: if you are willing to live the Christian life by following simple steps set forth by our Lord Himself, you will experience unconditional joy whether you win the lottery or lose your job. Pretty amazing, isn't it?

However, like all extravagant claims, there is a catch. You must have a problem of such magnitude that you are willing to go to any lengths to correct it. No problem, no joy. No willingness, no joy. Perhaps you are thinking these two statements are bizarre, or you may wonder what kind of problem I'm referring to. The soundness of the "no problem, no willingness" statements will become self-evident as you read. The bad news is that everyone has problems (Rom. 3:23). The good news is that by taking full responsibility for your troubles and applying these proven solutions, you will be delivered from your most chronic, seemingly hopeless problems as those very problems become motivational assets for living your new abundant life (2 Cor. 5:17). Clarification of the kinds of problems I'm referring to may be made by considering these additional questions:

- Do you have any behavior you've deemed necessary to change, but to no avail?
- Do you spend more time living in the past or the future than in the present?
- Do you eat, work, spend, worry, or play too much or do any of these things too little?
- Do you try to control people or circumstances, or does it too often seem as though these areas of your life are out of control?

➦ Are you frequently disappointed with yourself and/or others?

➦ Do you try to please others to the extreme, or are you not thoughtful enough?

➦ Are you always late, or are you obsessed with punctuality?

➦ Are you generally sad, depressed, or emotionally tired?

➦ Are your emotions primarily either "highs" or "lows"?

➦ Are you an egomaniac with an inferiority complex?

If you answer "yes" to any of these or similar questions, congratulations! If you are willing to follow the steps outlined in *The Promises* to correct any one or a combination of these problems, you are a prime candidate for unconditional joy.

I have found the suggestions and ideas on the following pages fascinating. More important, they have changed my life as I apply these eternal principles daily. It took me a lifetime to cultivate the troubles from which I sought relief in these principles. I must have come into this world with a low endorphin level. I don't know that my endorphin level has improved, but I have gradually come to experience unconditional joy. All it took was *willingness, one day at a time.* Are you willing? It won't be easy, but what could be simpler?

You will need to take this material slowly. It's not devotional, designed to tug at your heartstrings. Yet you will be amazed at how God will transform your "feelings" as a result of your doing the right actions. The repetitiveness of certain ideas and phrases is not accidental. Repetition is an effective feature of spiritual consciousness. I personally recall catchphrases throughout the day, every day. Nevertheless, even though you are encouraged to read and reread, at no point will it be necessary for you to understand the rationale for the things you will be asked to do.

You don't even have to have faith that the behavior set forth in the Beatitudes will work. Many followers began *The Promises* because they *had* to do something to change their lives. They were willing to do whatever it took, and although they didn't expect results, they were amazed that the concepts in this book worked for them. You must simply be *willing* to ascend each step in the order it is presented to the best of your ability. There you have it. You need only be willing, and God will provide the results. Now allow me to describe the origins of my amazing discovery.

In the 1930s, Bill Wilson, a hopeless alcoholic stockbroker, achieved sobriety by biblical principles introduced to him by a friend who had previously been Bill's fellow hopeless drinking partner. This friend had discovered these principles through participation in a back-to-the-basics, interdenominational fellowship known as the Oxford Group. Mr. Wilson (or Bill W. as he is known to fellow alcoholics) developed these principles into what is known today as the Twelve Steps of Recovery. These principles constitute the heart of Alcoholics Anonymous (AA), of which he is a cofounder. Prior to Mr. Wilson's inspiration, alcoholism was simply a fatal disease. Throughout history, with the few exceptions of dramatic spiritual conversions, the true alcoholic was destined for the isolation of an asylum, certain insanity, and/or a protracted death. With this backdrop, twelve-step recovery has provided hope to millions, and not just for alcoholics, but for many who suffer from a variety of mental disorders. It has provided solutions where religion, science, and medicine have failed.

When I was a seminary student, AA and the Twelve Steps surfaced frequently in pastoral care courses. Little did I know that these principles, which I tucked away for referral purposes in my forthcoming counseling practice, would unlock the door to simple self-evident truths that at the time, for whatever reason, did not seem all that relevant. I had professed Jesus Christ as my Lord and Savior at age nine, but it was not until age thirty-nine that, out of spiritual and emotional desperation, I became willing to apply these simple, tried-and-true principles in the vast spiritual wasteland of my own life. In my lifelong search for happiness, I discovered joy instead. I also discovered that, despite their generic structure, the Twelve Steps were practical adaptations of the teachings of Jesus in the Sermon on the Mount in general and the Beatitudes in particular. In his wisdom, Bill W. veiled these recovery principles from their biblical wellspring in order to make them palatable to even the most worldly-minded sufferer.

The spirituality advocated in the following pages is not intended to compete with or replace recovery programs based on the Twelve Steps. Rather, what I have done is to return, full circle, this natural progression of joy to its biblical home of origin. AA-style recovery involves twelve steps. As previously mentioned, the steps of the Beatitudes set forth here are referred to as *The Promises* and are seven in number. Each promise describes a level of spirituality and the behavior that characterizes it. If you are currently in twelve-step recovery, they contain nothing that would interfere with your progress. On the contrary, *The Promises* complement, support, and revitalize any spiritual pursuit. Hopefully you will find *The Promises,* which form the structure of this work, to be a helpful bridge between proven solutions to self-destructive behavior and the Divine Author from whom these solutions came.

Numerous counterfeit expressions of spirituality have flourished resembling the genuine article. For example, with Jesus' desert temptation experience as a precursor of His earthly ministry, meditation and contemplation have been fundamental and rich in the life of the church from its inception. Unfortunately, it has too often been relegated to a cloistered few. Meanwhile, its secular counterpart appears in the popular mainstream in various forms from Eastern religion, with a Christian vocabulary and New Age flair, to astrology and soothsaying. Unlike these counterfeit solutions and alluring options, the Beatitudes, as taught by our Lord, provide the real thing.

Choosing life in Christ is the most important decision you will ever make. One of your biggest challenges will be keeping your new life as simple as it really is. The following chapters are designed to anticipate some of the issues you will face in your spiritual progress. This entire spiritual program may be simply stated as follows.

Unconditional joy *"is God's will for you"* (1 Thess. 5:16, 18). You are created in the image of God, which means that there is a God-shaped space at the core of your being that only God can adequately fill. That space will be occupied, either by God or by your ego. The problems alluded to earlier are symptoms that your God-shaped space is inhabited by your ego. The way to both solve your problems and have unconditional joy is to deflate your cancerous ego, as God takes His rightful place at your core. This oneness with God is the purpose and goal of biblical spirituality. It is accomplished by God as you take the progressive steps laid out by Jesus in the Beatitudes. These steps are described and explained in the form of *The Promises*, which immediately follow this preface. It's as simple as that.

In order to help you stay focused on what you are about to do, a summary of the above paragraph, with diagrams to illustrate these concepts visually, is provided in the section entitled "Spirituality at a Glance." You are encouraged to consult this summary as you approach each chapter, or if you ever feel bogged down or overwhelmed.

Small specialty groups contribute to the life and ministry of many of today's most vibrant congregations. In order to apply *The Promises* more effectively in your life, you may want to join or establish a "Promise group" as a functional part of your church and pursue spiritual growth together. The section "Guidelines for Building a Promise Group" provides an outline for establishing such a group.

Also, as you undertake the practice of the principles, you will hopefully consult this material frequently. For me, this book is a true companion, second, of course, to its primary source, my Bible. To help you navigate in your daily study, the material is divided into two parts. Part One: P-Day (Preparation) is designed to help you break through denial and commit to a willingness to do the steps. Part Two: D-Day (Do) contains the steps themselves. These principles have a 100 percent success rate for all who give themselves fully to their practice. The preparatory material in Part One contains things that these "success stories" either had to come to grips with in order to give *The Promises* their full measure, or invaluable lessons they learned along the way.

If your denial has been shattered, and you are absolutely willing, you may be ready for D-Day, to dive right in. Even then, you will need to consult Part One as you go. Just as absolute willingness guarantees success, so anything less will guarantee failure. The choice is yours, but you will not go wrong if you pray for God's guidance.

I know the Beatitudes, *The Promises*, and the attitude of gratitude will bring you unconditional joy. I know because I have it, and I have it because, unless I am sleeping, I am practicing these principles. Believe me, I'm a strong-willed type who is normally easily frustrated and doesn't take instruction well. But at this modest stage of my spiritual development, doing these steps is not difficult at all. Rather, it is pure pleasure. Just as bad behavior perpetuates itself, so does good, healthy behavior. I don't always do it right, but God, not me, provides the results. I just do it! I hope that you will, too.

—GLENN W. NOWELL, PH.D., D.MIN.

The Promises

Our Lord and Savior Jesus Christ promises that we will experience divine joy, which is His will for us, to the extent that we take the following steps (Matt. 5:3–10):

1. We have joy admitting that we are powerless over sin, believing that only God can rescue and protect us, and *humbling* ourselves in all matters, trusting that, because of Him, ours is eternal life (Matt. 5:3).

2. We have joy *courageously evaluating our moral condition*, honestly admitting our immorality to God, facing it ourselves, and confessing it to another human being, trusting that we will experience an ongoing sense of well-being (Matt. 5:4).

3. We have joy *persevering* in the present, and seeking God's will and His power to accomplish it, trusting Him, rather than ourselves, for the results (Matt. 5:5).

4. We have joy doing whatever is necessary to *make amends*, in righting any wrong we have done to others, provided it is in their best interest, with no regard to any wrong they may have done to us, trusting that God will reward us with a deep sense of satisfaction (Matt. 5:6).

5. We have joy demonstrating *compassion* to all, knowing that even at our best, we, too, are in need of it, as we trust in God for His mercy (Matt. 5:7).

6. We have joy allowing our wills to be aligned with His to the point that our *motives* are *pure*, trusting that we will see God's active participation in our actions (Matt. 5:8).

7. We have joy pursuing *peace* and accepting *serenity* as the result of these steps, trusting that the Prince of Peace will declare us heirs of the kingdom (Matt. 5:9).

Our Lord promises that the practice of these principles will insure our joy in the midst of even the worst possible circumstances, for ours is eternal, abundant life (Matt. 5:10–12).*

*See page 202 for complete Scripture references.

Part One
PREP-DAY

(Preparation)

Chapter 1
Spirituality 101

66"**B**irds of a feather flock together." That was certainly true of the midweek Bible study where the group of young adults, several being parents of small children, looked alike, spoke alike, shared similar educational backgrounds, and to a real extent, thought alike. These genuinely good people bantered around Scripture dealing with the topic of forgiveness as they questioned whether it was possible, regarding certain transgressions, to both forgive *and* forget.

Just as they were about to agree that God is "realistic" about this matter, the only oddball in the group declared in a raspy voice, "Whenever I get upset or make a big deal of anything or anyone, other than God, I make a big deal of myself." This guy was older than the others, or at least he looked older. Unbeknown to the group, he was a recovered alcoholic. He was spouting good old-fashioned twelve-step lingo. That was the first and only thing he said. The group was very polite and accommodating with a moment of silence, followed by timid nods of approval. But, so as not to be derailed from the topic at hand, they returned undaunted to their original train of thought.

What was the old guy talking about? Was he self-absorbed and therefore missed the point of the discussion? Or could it be that the group missed the point of one of the most profound statements ever uttered? Was it possible that he was redefining the real issue of forgiveness?

Was the gentleman, weathered beyond his years, possibly establishing a framework for tapping into the very essence of spirituality?

It is difficult to accept or even recognize the profundity of this recovered alcoholic's statement because it smacks of something we would rather not hear. "Whenever I get upset or make a big deal of anything or anyone, other than God, I make a big deal of myself." Brace yourself. He was saying that whether you harbor a resentment, try to cope alone with a self-destructive child, isolate yourself because of deteriorating health, ruminate over an impending financial burden, or feel crushed because of rejection in an intimate relationship, *you* are your problem. Before you recoil, consider a truly wonderful upside of this discovery. Granted, you can't undo what has already happened. You can't, at least not in the long run, force people to behave a certain way. As much as you may be able to improve your physical health, eventually your body will deteriorate. **You can control you.** After all, everyone dies. And you certainly can't make people like or love you. If you are courageous enough to be brutally honest, you will admit that there is very little in your universe you can control. However, the upside is that you can control *you*. What a wonderful revelation!

The Christian is promised abundant life, one characteristic of which is unconditional joy. (See John 10:10; 1 Thessalonians 5:16.) Unfortunately, Christians have a track record of attempting to control the uncontrollable as much as their non-Christian neighbors. Even when we are convinced that we are acting selflessly, we are all clamoring to run the show while never receiving absolute cooperation from anyone. Although unconditional joy has always been a hallmark of biblical faith, it is no wonder that it remains a novel idea.

When trying to run your life, and the lives of everyone around you, the controls at your disposal are sort of like those of an iron-claw crane game in an arcade. You stand in front of the glass, deciding which toy to go for, but all your strategy will leave you fifty cents poorer. Regardless of how wise, submissive, or important you believe you are, if you are going to have an intimate relationship with God, you must relinquish your self-appointed position at the controls. This is not optional. It is a requirement. And what a wonderful requirement it is.

Why? Well, consider what "letting go" releases. The conviction that you need to be in control is as powerful in you as heroin is to the heroin addict. Where your relationship with God is concerned, it is also every bit as destructive. When you relinquish control, you let go of guilt, anger, needless stress, fear, and anxiety—and this is by no means an exhaustive list of the self-inflicted punishments from which you are released. You intentionally place all the important things in life in the hands of the One who is able to handle them. As frightening and impractical as turning over the reins to God may "feel," in doing so, you exchange the illusion of control for real power, energy-draining cycles for satisfying direction, and significant disappointments for a lifestyle of victories.

At this point, of course, this all sounds like theoretical, idealistic gobbledygook. Personal experience has taught you that theory, doctrine, devotional and inspirational material, biblical examinations of life issues, or a powerful sermon may make you think, but they cannot make you act upon the information no matter how theologically sound or motivating they are. You identify with the apostle Paul who described his own carnal nature this way:

> For I have the desire to do what is good, but I cannot carry it out. For what I do is not the good I want to do; no, the evil I do not want to do—this I keep on doing.
>
> (Rom. 7:18–19)

What makes the spirituality advocated here so radically different from what you have tried before? Answer: the principles contained in the Beatitudes and explained in *The Promises* (on page 16) are practical, measurable, gradual, and obtainable steps constituting a lifelong course of action with a guarantee of the specific result of unconditional joy set forth by none other than our Lord Himself. This material also provides other examples of Scripture in which God's will for you and your resulting well-being are identified, along with the corresponding course of action through which they may be obtained. This is miraculous information that has always been contained in God's Word.

Caution: biblical spirituality is not a technique. Positive thinking and positive self-talk are examples of many self-help techniques that are sound and very beneficial, but human techniques are not advocated here. Nor is this a program whereby you accomplish coping skills or a level of goodness to bring about your own salvation. This is not a method designed to draw God closer to you. All the positive results that you derive from the practice of these eternal principles are God's gift to you. God is the One who has initiated your relationship with Him, and He has provided you with the course of action you need in order to draw closer to Him. Again, this is not a program of your accomplishments. It is a program of ego deflation in which God fills the void left by a thorough housecleaning of the self-created clutter and debris that have kept you in denial, bondage, and separation from your Creator.

Counting the Cost

If you consider yourself a Christian, at what point did you count the cost of discipleship? If you are like most professing Christians, the cost to you as a follower of Jesus never entered your mind. You "accepted Jesus Christ" to get something, not to lose something. Perhaps you should have read Luke 14:25–33. Go ahead: check it out. Unfortunately, when it comes to relationships, human beings rarely count the cost. Without doing so, it is impossible to make a commitment. Without a commitment, significant relationships simply do not last. That is why marriages don't last, parents fail miserably, and Christians fizzle.

The following is an overview of what this program will require of you. This is your opportunity to count the cost. If you find this outline to be overwhelming, you may want to reread Luke 14:25–33. If you choose to take the words of Jesus in this passage seriously, the requirements of *The Promises* will be a walk in the park. Or, if you prefer a less dramatic way of approaching the following proposal, consider this challenge: if you will commit only a minute portion of the energy that you expend on preserving the current dysfunction in your life to this program, God will grant you unconditional joy. In other words, total commitment does not necessarily translate into expending more emotional energy than what you are now accustomed to.

So much of our skepticism is based on self-fulfilled prophecy. When people "fall" into marriage, they discover how flawed it is as an institution. When they juggle parenting with careers and the serious pursuits of leisure, entertainment, and self-actualization, they conclude that parenting is a no-win situation. And when people "try" Christianity, they prove to themselves how corrupt organized religion is. Honestly, marriage, parenthood, and organized religion are rewarding institutions. The core of the problem is always those who enter into these and other relationships without commitment.

Participants in twelve-step recovery often refer to their program saying, "It's not for those who *need* it; it's for those who *want* it." So it is with this program. If you want **Joy is for** to put your house in order, if you want solutions to your *living problems* (problems that **those who** have taken on a life of their own), and if you **want it.** want to have unconditional joy characterize your experience on this earth, you will find even the most challenging aspects of *The Promises* a small price to pay for the spiritual dividends you will receive both now and throughout eternity. There are no shortcuts to unconditional joy, but if you are willing to give yourself completely to each step of this program, there is nothing that can prevent God's gifts of grace, joy, and serenity from coming to you.

First, you will deal with some preliminary issues, including the defining of key terms. The foundation of general biblical principles will be established as a starting point so that we will be on the same page. You will be given advice on selecting a community of faith. Remember, nothing spiritual can be accomplished in isolation because, by definition, spirituality is all about relationships.

Much of this preliminary material will be theoretical. You will be given a lot to think about. Read and reread, but don't get bogged down. At any point, feel free to review "Spirituality at a Glance" to help reinforce a mental picture of what you are doing. Seek God's guidance and inspiration. You do not have to completely understand how this material works for it to produce God's intended miracles in your life. You **Simply do what the material says.** must simply *do* what the material says, and gradual understanding will be a by-product.

The bottom line is that *spiritual progress is not optional for the Christian.* Like the infant who either grows or dies, either you are an active participant in God's gift of salvation, or you have no salvation (James 20:20, 26). So you see, your conscious contact with God is a matter of eternal life or death. Feel-good group discussions and uplifting devotionals contribute to the maintenance of a robust life in Christ, but if you are in any way in a part-time relationship with God, you need to be immersed in *The Promises.*

Your first exercise is "counting the cost." Your second exercise will be to break through denial and face your problems. The third exercise will be a real treat. You will practice the attitude of gratitude. The apostle Paul provided a "formula" for how to *"be joyful always"* in 1 Thessalonians 5:16–18. Like everything else in this program, you will have to dive in headfirst and just do it in order to experience the results. Although most people are grateful for especially good things that come their way, few have the experience of a mind-set of gratitude. By consistently acting upon a regimen of realistic evaluation of the many details of your life, including those you would normally consider obstacles to happiness, you will develop a new nature filled with joy, regardless of what life throws at you. Your attitude of gratitude will provide you with the perfect mind-set to approach *The Promises*.

Beginning with chapter 4, you will find introductory material, including a rationale for the construction of *The Promises* and an illustration of how these steps were the conduits of a miracle in the lives of a couple whose relationship appeared hopeless. From chapter 5 on, you will set in motion the practice of one Promise or Beatitude at a time. You will be surprised at how undaunting the tasks are. The combination of soothing and powerful results of your labor, which you will clearly recognize as gifts bestowed from God, will reinforce each step of your spiritual and behavioral progress.

Frank's Story

God's Promises provide solutions to practically any human living problem. For introductory purposes, it was tempting to illustrate this transforming power in a setting of an obvious problematic condition, such as obesity or rage. There are plenty of examples of recovery from such problems, the process would be easy to follow, and the results would be dramatic. Unfortunately, life is usually not that clear-cut. To appreciate the following case study, there is a particularly baffling obstacle with which you will have to contend. You will face it in counting the cost of your relationship with Jesus Christ. It will obstruct your vision of your self-image, and it will be a key determining factor in whether you are willing to give yourself entirely to this program. It is the relentless problem of *denial*.

You see, most people sincerely believe that their problems are caused by circumstances or influences outside themselves, and they can point to an endless array of proofs to reinforce this conviction. All the while, the reality is that most of our problems are of our own making. An obvious example is the guy who is convinced that he drinks because of a rotten job and failed marriage, when in reality these two crucial areas of his life have run amuck because of his drinking. The obvious truth in this illustration is easy to spot by those of us on the outside looking in, but the practicing alcoholic can't see it and is convinced that if you can, you just don't understand.

To the casual observer, Frank was a picture of emotional and physical health. Even the pre-transformed Frank is the sort of fellow many of us would be proud to have as a son. We tend to see people like Frank as more in need of coping skills than of a complete spiritual overhaul. If we look closely enough, we see an accomplished professing Christian, who, like many of us, has had great success performing under his own direction and power. Also, like many of us, Frank judges others by their actions while he evaluates himself by a sincere, but distorted, view of his motives. Although Frank offers us little information about how *The Promises* provided a solution to his self-centered condition, he gives a host of tiny sparkling gems of wisdom that will gradually illuminate our own experiences as we take the narrow, unbeaten path of abundant life upon which Frank is well on his way.

It has been suggested that in order for someone to benefit from a step program, one must "hit bottom." Well, Frank's "bottom" hit at a level where most of his achievements remained intact; and yet, his spiritual bankruptcy was as serious and motivating to him as the loss of a marriage, job, or health might be to someone else. It may surprise you, as it surprised Frank, that you can choose the floor at which you exit the down elevator. Hitting bottom, without the willingness

You can choose the floor at which you exit.

to take the necessary steps for transformation, is nothing more than the pathetic endurance of tragedy. On the other hand, when hitting bottom becomes a person's springboard for salvation, a problem-riddled past becomes one of the greatest assets for living the Christian life. Let us now examine the many facets of Frank's transforming experiences.

The Story (as told by Frank)

My buddies and I used to joke about the military retirees on base. They were easy to spot as volunteers in the hospital, congesting the aisles and checkout lines at the Commissary, and setting up shop every morning in front of the Base Exchange with specialty items, some as ridiculous as porcelain statues of famous sports figures. I mean, where would anyone put a porcelain statue of Lee Trevino? We made light of the polyester pants, the cream-colored walking shoes, and the baseball caps that read "Twice as Much Husband on Half as Much Pay." They just couldn't cut the umbilical cord, couldn't let go. Now that I'm a retiree myself, I see things quite differently. I applaud them for making the most of their past and present. They make a hospital stay a little bit brighter. The Sunday school, organizations, and the congregation at the base chapel are like a parade with active duty personnel passing through. Retirees provide continuity, the glue that helps hold these groups together and keeps them going. Now that I'm one of them, I realize that the happiest retirees are the ones who give the most. As far as I'm concerned, they can dress any way they want.

I retired as a "full-bird" colonel and wing commander. Had it not been for a spiritual awakening, I believe that I would have retired in total despair at not having been selected to the rank of general officer. I was always an overachiever. You might say that I was an egomaniac with an inferiority complex. I never quite accepted life on life's terms. I guess I was no different from many teenagers in that I always felt like everyone else had a little better handle on life. I lettered in football and basketball, although I had neither the weight nor the height to be the most valuable player in either sport—an early example of a lifelong stream of frustrations and disappointments. However, I was proud of my academic prowess. I would have liked to graduate from high school as the valedictorian, but I was pleased with my 3.9 grade point average, which qualified me for an appointment to the Air Force Academy.

I guess you could say that in order to feel as good as everyone else, I had to be better than everyone else. It wasn't a very happy way to live, but this general dissatisfaction with life and a passion to overachieve proved to be a consistent driving force for one success after another. I graduated with distinction from the academy, I was at the head of the class in pilot training, and from my very first assignment, I was considered a "fast-burner." I might not have been comfortable with life in general, but I was doing something I loved. As a child I had built a room full of model airplanes. Now I was living my childhood fantasies.

I not only wanted to achieve more than others, but also wanted to be morally better than others. I was one of those rare kids who stayed away from alcohol and marijuana. I was the natural leader of our church youth. At the academy we marched to chapel, but after graduation I continued to be active in church. I was a baptized, membership-holding, "born-again" Christian. I met my wife, Sarah, in an adult singles group of the local church just as I was receiving orders for my second assignment. Madly in love and unable to imagine life without one another, we managed to have all of a two-month engagement that culminated with a wedding in the church where we had met. Part of the haste, as we rationalized it, was motivated by the military regulations requiring marriage in order to be eligible for family base housing upon arrival at the new assignment.

You might say a short courtship couldn't be helped. Also beyond our control, the first of our three adorable children was born a month and a half into my first remote assignment in Greenland. Sarah was completely devoted to the children, and whether at home or away, I considered myself to be a thoroughly devoted husband and father, taking on increased responsibilities at work and securing a bright career of which the family could be proud. I guess all professions reward their workaholics well. That was certainly the case with the Air Force. But I not only gave the Air Force my best, I gave my church my best. So did Sarah and the kids. Whenever possible, we were there as a family. Sarah and I both taught Sunday school, and the children's religious education became as much a priority as other aspects of their lives. We believed that a family that prays together stays together. We were not together nearly as much as any of us would have liked, but we did pray together and have sit-down meals as a family whenever possible.

Neither Sarah nor I would have settled for anything less than a Christian partner in life. I appreciated Sarah's devotion to the children and to my career. She was a natural in heading up the officers' wives' club. Considering her preparation and my fast-track progression through the ranks, it was no surprise that, when I was selected for the position of Wing Commander, she took her place as the commander's wife. The figurative eagles she wore on her designer clothes were as large and shiny as mine. However, she never seemed to appreciate her status in the base community or my devotion to her and the kids as a hardworking husband and father. In fact, it seemed as though the more blessed we became, the farther apart we grew. Sarah's critical, unappreciative attitude also took its toll on the children. As they grew older they became experts in dumping guilt on me for not spending enough time with them, and then, when I did set aside what little time was available to do something they wanted to do, they would have other plans.

To top it off, there was a serious accident on the flight line with one of my squadrons that was completely beyond my control. Even though I was cleared across the board of any responsibility, because the accident occurred on my watch, I had effectively reached the height of my career. My chances of becoming a flag officer were dashed, Sarah was on the verge of demanding legal separation, and the kids acknowledged my presence only in passing. In my early forties, I found myself on medication for high blood pressure. I felt spiritually numb and sure that I had wasted the best years of my life on a host of "ingrates," from my superiors at work to my youngest, once-adoring child. If anyone deserved a midlife crisis, I did. I landed in deep depression. Had my life turned out any better than those of some of my adulterous, hell-raising peers? What about all this business of "seek ye first the kingdom" and all that other stuff "will be added unto you"? (See Matthew 6:33.) I had "been there, done that," and it didn't work! In reality, despite my sincerity, sharp intellect, and wise judgment, I had not been there, nor had I done that. Perhaps I can best explain what I mean by describing what happened next.

Seeking help was one of the hardest things I've done. After all, I was the Wing Commander. Everyone knew me. All the health service agencies on base worked for me. I couldn't go to Mental Health on base and risk having it in my record. My record had already been tarnished by something from which I'd been completely exonerated. The Senior Chaplain was a member of my staff and a personal friend. For most of my assignments, my family and I had been members of a civilian church, but we were currently active in the base chapel because, as Wing Commander, I felt it my obligation to support the chapel community on base. Besides, I was an ordained Baptist deacon who wouldn't have wanted his pastor to know how bad things had gotten. Under the guise of referring a confidential situation in one of the squadrons to that squadron's chaplain, I, a colonel, bared my soul to a chaplain who, of all people, was a captain. I was surprised, to say the least, when he called me on my little charade of seeking help for another, but his focus on getting all the cards on the table was just what I needed.

I proceeded to describe to the chaplain how unfair the whole world had become, which for me consisted of my spouse and children, and the Air Force, and not particularly in that order. It was refreshing to vent my anger about a host of adversarial relationships while this captain respectfully listened, keeping any self-righteous judgments to himself. I realized as I spoke that I really wasn't interested in help, whatever that might have been. I needed a sounding board, and he was it. As I was wrapping up the sordid details with no intentional plans of a follow-up, he interrupted with a rather crude assessment of what he thought my problem was. He said, "You know, Colonel, you've got several addictions that are driving the despair you are experiencing." I thought to myself, "What the heck is he talking about?"

"What do you mean by addictions? Addictions to what?" I demanded. He responded calmly, "By addiction, I mean the way the word is usually used. You're addicted to work, for one. Then there is perfection, control, and with time, I'm sure we can come up with some others." Before I could contain myself I blurted out in a disagreeing and rejecting tone, "Is that bad?" The fact was, I rather passionately considered hard work, perfection, and exercising self-control and control over one's environment as virtues for which to strive. I thought to myself, these are the virtues that made me the man I am today. It was as though this guy was in cahoots with the rest of the screwed-up world. Surely a man of the cloth recognized when someone was trying to do good.

It turned out that I was only partly correct. These qualities had greatly influenced who I had become. The chaplain carefully wove my own observations into his assessment of me. He turned on enough heat to keep my attention, but not so much as to run me off. Also, early on in that first conversation, he put to rest the perception that he was talking down to me by sharing with me what he called "predispositions," or addictive tendencies, in his own behavior.

Without getting bogged down into details, during the months that followed, the chaplain helped me identify the real problems in my life and what to do about them. I learned that my basic problem was with something I had in common with everyone, which is self-centeredness. That meant instead of wasting energy trying to control and correct people and circumstances around me, my focus needed to be on the one and only thing that I could control—me. I learned that my pride, false self-confidence, and egocentric behavior were cover-ups for low self-esteem. Imagine *me* with low self-esteem. I learned that even in my lowest mental and spiritual state, I had an infinite list of reasons to be grateful to God, and that the act of identifying these reasons, in and of itself, dramatically changed for the better my suffering mental and spiritual state.

I had an infinite list of reasons to be grateful to God.

I learned that there were very few things, like work, perfection, or control, that were bad or even negative, in and of themselves. So-called "addictive agents" realized their potential for evil "when they were used as the manipulative, counterfeit substitutes for a relationship with God." That was one of those tongue-tying phrases the chaplain used. In other words, it's anything I try to get from someone or something that I can really get only from God. I learned that sin was a lot more complicated than I had ever thought and that the solution to sin was a lot simpler than I had ever imagined.

As a born-again Christian, I believed that Christ had paid the price for my sins and that turning to Him as my Lord and Savior was the only way to bridge the gap between me and God. But I still held to the notion, to use the chaplain's words, that I could somehow "manipulate or flirt with sin, yet go unscathed." In fact, when I took what the chaplain called "a personal moral inventory," I discovered quite a few character defects I had nurtured and was willing to protect at all cost. In fact, these character defects and personal excesses were so fundamental to who I had gradually and unwittingly become as a person; conventional religious alternatives like consistent church attendance, teaching Sunday school, singing in the choir, tithing, and participating in Bible study groups seemed to have little real substantive impact on my basic self-centeredness. I always felt better when I did these things. Yet, in some ways, the closer I walked the straight and narrow, the more critical and judgmental I became of others. I still craved personal recognition for my good deeds, and the more time and money I invested in the church, the more sensitive and quick to take things personally I became.

Up until the occurrence of the accident on the flight line, at least my day job as an officer and a gentleman seemed more manageable, predictable, and immediately rewarding than my spiritual and personal life. While my wife and kids never fully appreciated me, up until now the Air Force had appropriately rewarded me for faithful service. My work had become the only thing I could depend on, and now, even it had pulled the rug out from under me.

The chaplain introduced me to what he called "the joy of appreciating paradox." The paradox that I was beginning to appreciate was that all these painful tragedies, like the family rejecting me, the negative career impact of the flight line accident, and my overall sense of depression and despair, were occasions that brought me back to where I belonged in the first place as a follower of Christ. It brought me to my knees with a willingness to humble myself and recognize my absolute dependence upon God. And, in consistent paradox fashion, in this newfound dependence and humility, I began to experience a level of joy I had never dreamed possible.

It's a long, frightening fall from Wing Commander to my new officially retired status. The final chapter is closed on my beloved Air Force career. I am adjusting one day at a time to putting God first, my family second, and me third.

Who knows, I may eventually learn to love my neighbor as I love myself. Of course, first I have to learn how to love myself, which is quite different from my track record of putting myself first. My wife, Sarah, loves change. I, on the other hand, have always hung on desperately to the status quo. Despite this long list of potentially painful adjustments I am currently undergoing, indeed, in the actual act of undergoing them, I am experiencing a deep sense of joy and personal satisfaction. It's because it's all part of being in Christ, as opposed to being in myself. **Humility is a** To quote my chaplain advisor, "humility (a **wonderful** basic ingredient of being in Christ) doesn't mean you think less of yourself, you just **way to live.** think of yourself less." He has lots of good ones like that, which he's passed along to me from others. I know it sounds strange, but humility is a wonderful way to live.

By the way, remember the "Twice as Much Husband on Half as Much Pay" hat? Well, my family is getting a lot more husband and father than they've ever had. It's amazing how when I work on myself, those around me get better. I have what the chaplain calls a "seven-step road map of self-imposed behavior modification." Each step is based on the one before it, and I am at the point where I am in some way practicing just about all of them every day. When I work 'em, they work, and when they work, I have the joy of focusing on the really important things. Once I took that first step, it became a lot more natural than I thought it would be to practice these principles. When I do get off track, and I do more than I would like to admit, it's as though I revert to my old ways instantly. But after tasting this new way of living spiritually, motivation to stay on track is not a problem.

I was asked to share my story as a sort of introduction to the Christian life as set forth by our Lord in the Sermon on the Mount. I know that these principles work, and not just for people like me. I've learned much about these joy-inspiring principles from recovering spouse abusers, people with eating disorders, people who at one time spent their way into bankruptcy or prison, divorcees who swore they would never love again, recovering people who are physically or mentally challenged as the result of substance abuse, recovering religious fanatics, and people of all ages and economic status. One thing we all have in common with each other and all people is the need to get out of ourselves and into Christ. Make no mistake, we have no illusion that we are earning our salvation or that we are capable in any way of doing so. However, knowing that God is eternally unwavering in nurturing His part of His relationship with us, we are merely seeking to do our best to uphold our part of the relationship. This requires that we do certain things that we don't have to figure out, spiritually discern, or wait to have revealed. They are set forth as various levels of Christian growth in the Beatitudes.

I would like to thank Dr. Nowell for sharing my story. I am deeply grateful for the honor of its use as an introduction to a practical guide in applying the Beatitudes to everyday life. By the way, I am currently being offered an excellent job with an aircraft company. However, I have no desire to relocate, and thanks to my newfound relationship with Christ, accepting the position as a means of restoring self-worth or insuring financial security no longer determines my decision-making process. God's will, as Sarah, the kids, and I understand it, will determine our decision. Until then, I hope my friends with the cream-colored walking shoes feel comfortable around me with my cross-trainers, because I'm on my way to the hospital to do some volunteering.

Chapter 2
Things You Need to Know

Regarding your spiritual condition, there's good news and there's bad news. The bad news is that, at best, life is short and if you keep on doing whatever you're doing or living however you're living, it won't get better. It will get worse. Getting religion or giving lip service to Christianity will not improve your condition one bit. The good news is that the following material will empower you to accurately diagnose your spiritual condition and, more important, it will provide you with practical solutions that God Himself guarantees will work. Furthermore, you will be able to enjoy the results of abundant life almost immediately. Please remember this when you reread lines to get their full import. What a small price for getting what you have always wanted! (If you aren't exactly sure what you've always wanted, the section "Why Settle for Happiness?" may help.)

Until now you have always thought of your problems as aggravations to your general quality of life or, in some cases, as horrible threats to your very existence. Perhaps you only thought of problems when they were obstacles you could not avoid. Or maybe your obsession with an actual or perceived problem *was* your problem. Now you are going to experience your problems in a fascinating and encouraging way. First John 1:9 says, *"If we confess our sins, he is faithful and just and will forgive us our sins and purify us from all unrighteousness."* This is a succinct way of saying, if you are willing to identify and own the dreaded messes you have made, God will transform your repentant action into a conduit of spiritual wholeness. The very parts of your history that repelled you most, the skeletons in your closet, and the occasions of guilt and shame you pretend never happened, will become great assets—spoils of victory—as God empowers you to be a redeeming force for others.

In this chapter you will learn what a *real* problem is and what your own personal problems are, so you will know what to work on. You will come to know the difference between happiness and joy in order to know what you are working toward. And you will be introduced to the proposition that you do not have to completely understand *The Promises*, the method by which you will face and solve your problems, in order to put them into practice or experience their miraculous results. Note that this chapter is entitled "Things You Need to Know." It is not entitled "Things You Need to Understand."

What's Your Problem?

In the New Testament the Greek noun for sin is *hamartia* (John 8:21; Rom. 3:9; 1 Cor. 15:17; 1 Thess. 2:16). The verb is *hamartano* (Matt. 27:4; Titus 3:11; Heb. 3:17, 10:26; 1 John 1:10). The Scriptures listed above are but a few examples of the attention God's Word devotes to the topic of sin. And no wonder. Sin is so baffling and powerful that it separates you from God and leads to death. The literal definition of these Greek words is "to miss the mark."

Of course, the biblical concept of sin has developed far beyond that. The implication is that God has established a bull's-eye, and anything less than hitting it is sin. This root definition lends itself well to the popular notion that "we all make mistakes." A blatant tip of the iceberg of denial that exists throughout our society is that when people own up to an unwanted pregnancy, cheating on a test, or having an affair, they admit to a "mistake."

Furthermore, people have come to believe that taking "full responsibility" is merely a matter of recognizing their destructive actions. In order to minimize consequences, one simply sinks deeper into denial in which serious flaws and character defects are considered "normal."

There are consequences for everything we do, good and evil. God holds no one responsible for mistakes, but mistakes contain their own inherent consequences. Depending on the circumstance, the consequence may be horrendous. But the fact is, sin is everywhere while mistakes are few and far between. Calling the wrong number is a mistake. Having information overheard by the wrong party while confiding in a supportive friend is a mistake. Throwing yourself into your work at the expense of your family is not a mistake. Intimidating people with rage because it consistently gets the desired results is not a mistake. Using an illness to control other family members is not a mistake. These, as with all sins, are self-centered acts that perpetrate evil.

There are no victimless crimes. Situation ethics have muddied the waters, but the ingredients, right and wrong, are still present in the mixture. Situation ethics rationalize; therefore, the situation ethics system is a perfect fit for the humanistic, self-centered mind. For example, few people think of abortion as a good thing. However, if it is *your* daughter in high school who becomes pregnant, the rationalizing human mind may consider it "the lesser of two evils."

What are the two evils? Well, she could bring the baby to term, but we all know who would end up raising the child. Even if she did step up to the plate, taking on the role of single mother would shatter her prospects of a bright future. After nine months of bringing the baby to term, could she give it up for adoption? In the case of a closed adoption, how could she be happy knowing nothing about the child's fate? The other option is to abort the child. Here the brilliance of the rationalizing mind comes to the forefront. We reason that the unborn child, especially in the early stages of development, is not a child at all. It is a fetus, or more accurately, a tissue mass. Women discharge fertilized eggs frequently without being aware of it. If the abortion is administered early enough, it will be hardly more painful than some of the routine discomforts of pregnancy. Most important, the teen's quality of life will remain intact. Following a practically unnoticeable absence, she will barely miss a beat in her social and academic life. She will have learned a valuable lesson from her "mistake." Why should an unwanted child be thrust into the world, anyway? The procedure must be done because it is the "fair" choice for everyone involved (except for the one receiving the death penalty), and therefore it must be right.

When the rationalizing human mind functions as its own highest authority, it selects what is real and what is not, not unlike the various forms of insanity. When it rejects or overlooks the boundaries established in God's Word, the entire evaluative process becomes flawed. You see, biblical truth is not simply true because the Bible says it; the Bible says it *because it is true.* The rationalized decision in our illustration ignored the fact that the pregnancy was not a mistake. It was a *consequence* of an act of transgression whereby an immature, irresponsible, ill-equipped, and uncommitted child intentionally flirted with a dangerous pleasure, thinking that she would, in all probability, go unscathed. She ignored the sacredness of the sexual act. The decision to abort circumvented the sanctity of life by reinventing the biology of the fetus. And because the decision was one of convenience, it considered primarily surface issues and appearance. More careful consideration would have revealed that rarely does a woman ever, during the course of her lifetime, recover from the emotional scars of aborting her child, regardless of her ethical, ideological, or religious value system. Likewise, cases of women expressing regret at any point in their lives for bringing an unwanted pregnancy to term are practically non-existent.

We all make mistakes, and we can learn from our mistakes. We all sin; and yes, we can learn and profit from our evil choices and behavior. This is where, when it comes to our relationship with God and with our fellow human beings, we can choose to be on the front line of victory, even over our worst transgressions. The most guilt-ridden veteran of multiple abortions can, for example, experience ego deflation, incredible self-esteem, and *unconditional joy*. These wonderful qualities can characterize her life, not by suppressing her evil choices or by putting them "behind her," but by embracing them, confessing them, trusting God to forgive them, and doing whatever is in the realm of her ability to make amends to all parties involved. When we are willing to take God's principles seriously in our lives, all things are possible. (See Mark 9:23; 10:27.)

Sin, the Down Escalator

One of the many horrible things about sin is its tendency to escalate. For example, a person tells a lie to cover for a previous one. Before the person knows it, he or she is "living a lie." Some people are compulsive liars and lie for no apparent reason. Either condition may lead to full-blown addiction. At this point behavioral science confirms what the Bible has always maintained. Sin works—it provides a shortcut to a desired result, it provides the illusion of control, and if unchecked, it will gain control of its host. (See Genesis 3.)

A popular TV commercial for potato chips said, "Nobody can eat just one." That's the way sin is. No one lies just once. No one flirts with sex just once. No one experiments with drugs just once. The Samaritan woman at the well did not have one single affair. She was living with a man who was not her husband, and she'd had five husbands before him. (See John 4:1–42.) In first-century Jewish and Samaritan cultures, a woman's survival was dependent upon her relationship to a man. If she was not married, she required the care of her father, brother, or some other male relative, or she prostituted herself. Surely, in the Samaritan woman's mind, circumstances warranted her illegitimate relationships.

Satan is cunning and crafty. His broadest theater of operation of spiritual warfare is not in the seedy places of the underworld. It is in the realm of morally neutral and virtuous activities. For example, the Bible warns against the evils of laziness. (See Ecclesiastes 10:18; Matthew 25:26.) No one argues that laziness is good, but neither is working too hard. Yet we reward and honor the workaholic. We saw this in "Frank's Story," and it is no doubt true of most successful people, including well-known pastors. The cold, hard fact is that workaholism affects its host and the family in much the same way as does alcoholism. In many cases, workaholics and alcoholics have similar life spans and promote similar dysfunctional family behavior. The workaholic may suffer from hypertension while the alcoholic battles liver disease. When it comes to the needs of the family, neither the workaholic nor the alcoholic is there. Both generate anger and resentment in the ones who are supposed to be most important to them. And both will go to bizarre lengths to maintain their denial.

Only God can forge steps of behavior that will more than adequately address sin from its most blatant violent form to its more cunning, cancerous type. Individual sinful acts are but symptoms of the deeper problem of self-centeredness. The Beatitudes treat the whole person. Living problems are addressed at their root. Identifying, confessing, and even repenting of blatant sins, for most of us, are not nearly as difficult as addressing our sinful nature, which constitutes the heart of our chronic, dysfunctional living problems.

Sin has been defined. Scripture develops it far beyond its root meaning of "missing the mark." Failing to hit the bull's-eye may well be a mistake, but your problems are not your mistakes. Your problems are not even your one-time sins. They are your chronic, self-destructive behaviors. These are the behaviors the Beatitudes will address. Allowing God to remove these behaviors from you will be your confirmation of God's grace. As you immerse yourself in *The Promises,* the very behaviors that separated you from God will be transformed into motivating allies in your intimate communion with God.

Problems are chronic, self-destructive behavior.

As you come to terms with your living problems, the following clarifications will help:

1. Let us distinguish between *living problems* and just plain problems. If a hairstylist cut off more hair than you requested, that is a problem. If you obsess about the damage throughout the day, or if you continue to carry a resentment toward the hairstylist, that is a living problem.

2. The plural of *problem* is used, because rarely does a person struggle with a single living problem. Problems beget problems, and a major living problem is usually the symptom of a variety of interrelated problems.

3. Denial is such a powerful obstacle that *willingness* is crucial when admitting problems as well as when applying solutions.

4. Proven solutions are those that are time-tested, measurable, and applicable by most people regardless of their intelligence or emotional stability.

The following list provides examples of living problems. The list is in no way exhaustive. In fact, it barely scratches the surface. It is hoped that these examples will stir your thinking as you seek to identify your own problems. If you are honest and thorough, you will no doubt be able to either add to this list or be much more specific in your own case than these broad categories.

- Anger that routinely escalates to rage
- Abusive, destructive relationships, whether victim or perpetrator
- Excessive need for control, particularly in the family, job, or private environment
- Persistent financial problems, including excessive shopping and/or overspending
- Overeating, anorexia, bulimia, or other eating disorders
- Addiction to gambling, sex, or sports
- Hypochondria
- Obsessive attention to health, physical conditioning, or outward appearance
- Focusing on religious rules or formulas at the expense of healthy spirituality
- Substance abuse or addiction
- Workaholism
- Dependency upon pleasing people, or the opposite extreme: giving little regard to the needs or wishes of others
- Obsessive-compulsive disorder, including handwashing, organizing, cleaning, checking, or ruminating

The list is open-ended. Some of these problems are very embarrassing and require great amounts of energy in order to maintain secrecy. The isolation they encourage further ingrains them into our personalities. It is interesting to note that most of these elements are, in and of themselves, either neutral as to their moral value, or are in fact good. For example, we would all do well to exercise and strive to maintain a healthy diet. However, some people are so obsessed with exercise and health foods that their ability to perform in a functional environment is dramatically restricted. With denial as a key ingredient, even the worthiest pursuits sometime very gradually escalate into full-blown attachments or addictions. In fact, in the 1990 Thomas Nelson publication of the *Serenity New Testament*, Drs. Robert Hemfelt and Richard Fowler referred to these conditions as "addictive agents." Whether you think of them as addictions or not, your primary challenge at this point is to recognize and admit your living problems. This is such a baffling obstacle that, if you are willing to do this, you will experience your first miracle in this program.

Recovery or the Christian Life?

For a program designed to minimize the ego and promote humility, it would be presumptuous and arrogant to claim that *The Promises* are for everyone if it were not for the fact that they are simply commentary from the Beatitudes and related Scripture, that the Beatitudes contain the essence of the Christian life, and that salvation through Jesus Christ is offered to all. The biblical principles offered here for you to follow have been tried and proven true for centuries. They are not just some new discovery that might work for you. That is why the bold claims are made that (1) they provide solutions to practically any living problem, and (2) these solutions benefit anyone capable of applying them. That is why, although the similarities between the Twelve Steps and *The Promises* are striking, it is made clear in "The Must-read Preface" that this biblical approach is not designed to compete with or replace *recovery* programs.

Recovery programs have a singular purpose, such as overcoming the abuse of a particular substance, an eating disorder, and so on. Jesus' Beatitudes address any living problem. However, there is also a distinction between the two in that *recovery* carries with it the notion of *restoration*. Many of us who desire a personal relationship with Jesus Christ as our Lord and Savior have never been in a healthy place to which to be "restored." For us, a program of action based on the Beatitudes is the Christian life set forth in its true simplicity, presented in bite-sized chunks for human consumption at all levels of spiritual growth and discipleship.

The Promises provide the absolute best, most joyful, and, in the long run, easiest way to live. But in choosing this new life in Christ, you must first be willing to break through denial by identifying your living problems. Next, you must decide whether or not they constitute behavior that is unacceptable to you. Others may consider certain aspects of your behavior to be chronic and/or unacceptable, but until *you* consider the behavior unacceptable, there will be no solutions to your living problems.

Denial is so powerful that it is amazing how even the most well-intentioned of us will embrace routine self-destructive behavior as being fundamental to who we are until we would not dream of living without it. To attack the particular behavior is to attack our personality defects, which in turn is to attack the person we are, which is to attack our *ego,* the most rudimentary, cherished part of our being. Regarding this dilemma, the genius of *The Promises* is that they "attack" nothing. Once we have identified our living problems and deemed them unacceptable to us, we merely take the first step of the Christian life, which is first admitting that we are powerless over the threatening behavior and then believing that only God can rescue and protect us from it. We do not attempt to fight, manipulate, or adjust the behavior. Instead, God meets us at the point of our willingness to let go of our sins, as He replaces the void left by the letting go with the indescribable sense of well-being of His presence.

Are the Beatitudes Really for Everyone?

God's principles for living are universal. For the Christian, the Beatitudes are to the New Testament what the Ten Commandments are to the Old. However, the three most common objections to this claim of universality are: (1) What about the person who is mentally or physically impaired to the point that he or she is incapable of doing what the principles require? (2) Is a steady diet of ego deflation healthy in extreme cases of low self-esteem? (3) What about disorders that require medication?

The answer to the first question is simple. People who are incapable of distinguishing between right and wrong are not held accountable for their actions. Perhaps only God knows to what extent a person whose brain is fried from substance abuse is responsible, but that person's case is far different from the individual whose brain never developed to competency in the first place. In any case, God does not hold people responsible for things they are not responsible for.

The second objection regarding cases of low self-esteem includes the person who whines and is always negative or critical, the individual who subconsciously seeks out abusive relationships, and the poor soul with no self-confidence whose repeated defeats are self-fulfilled prophecies. Wouldn't ego deflation be counterproductive or devastating to such people? The answer is no. These people are prime candidates for *The Promises* because their pathetic lives result from self-centeredness to the extreme. The deeper into dysfunction they sink, the more it affects everything around them. They are a classic example of how ego inflation is capable of minimizing self-esteem to the danger point. The worst case scenario is the person who loses the will to live. Self-destruction and suicide are incompatible with the mind intimately and selflessly bound to God.

This leads to the third concern of the appropriateness of applying spiritual solutions to cases that clearly require medical treatment. The answer is that it would be irresponsible to avoid utilizing the truly God-given medical discoveries that have been proven, in many cases, to effectively treat the chemical imbalances of those who suffer from such maladies as obsessive-compulsive and bipolar disorders, clinical depression, schizophrenia, and various forms of neuroses and psychoses. However, all these debilitating illnesses, by their very nature, feature an isolating self-centeredness. Medication can provide relief, but only God can restore wholeness. Likewise, just as medication must be taken on a consistent basis, so a person's relationship with God requires consistent maintenance. God, of course, is the Author and Sustainer of our healthy relationship with Him. However, our ego-driven nature requires that we apply His principles in our lives in order to maintain a receptiveness of His gift of that relationship and its resulting holistic health.

An angry, selfish, unethical, manic-depressive personality may obtain chemical balance through prescribed medications, but unless the spiritual condition is addressed, he or she is likely to remain an angry, selfish, unethical, "recovering" person. Or, as a recovering alcoholic recalled his personality when he stopped drinking before he immersed himself in the spiritual program of Alcoholics Anonymous, "As a drunk, I was a real so-and-so. When I stopped drinking, I became a sober so-and-so." As a matter of fact, because the thinking process is burdensome enough for people with mental disorders, the emphasis upon prescribed, somewhat regimented actions as set forth in this program makes it well suited for anyone who suffers. Suffice it to say, biblical spirituality offers solutions for anything to anyone who is capable and willing to undertake them.

Few are capable of applying the principles of this program in large chunks. No one is capable of applying them all at once in the beginning. That is why God provided us with solutions in the form of simple and specific steps to be taken gradually, one day at a time. These steps are so basic that often even people with severe mental disorders can apply them. In fact, the severity of the disorder can actually serve as a catalyst in the development of a willingness to apply these steps. The bottom line is that if you are willing to recognize and admit to the problems in your life and are willing to do something about them, you are now ready to proceed.

You Don't Have to Understand

If you invested in the most elaborate computer you could afford and committed yourself to hours of exploration of its limitless possibilities, that computer's owner's manual would probably be one of the most important and interesting books on your shelf. However, if you had that same manual, but no computer, or if you were merely interested in becoming computer literate, that manual would be dry, difficult to understand, or perhaps useless to you. So it is with this material. Either you have, for whatever reasons, the desire and willingness to do whatever it takes to step up to the quality of life that is both God's will for you and is full of unconditional joy, or you feel relatively secure with where you are.

If the first is the case, you should become accustomed to rereading and consulting the portions of this material that apply to the particular spiritual level you are concentrating on. If this material becomes tedious, nonsensical, or boring, you may in fact fit the second category, in which case you may question whether you are ready to proceed. It is not your job to work up the motivation to move forward with this program. God will provide the motivation. He will use your living problems as a catalyst. You must simply be willing to recognize your problems for what they are. You can see how important breaking through denial is to this or any program of spirituality.

God will provide the motivation.

While you determine your motivation for pursuing an intimate relationship with God, you do not have to understand the material itself or how it works. If you are committed to following the principles, it is simply not necessary to understand them in order to do them. *The Promises* provide concrete, measurable, and obtainable applications of behavior. You follow the directives of God, the steps explain how to do it, and God provides results that will soon become obvious to you and others. God empowers you, through this program, to turn the tables on the most addictive, dysfunctional, and self-destructive of forces. The more self-destructive and ingrained the behavior, the greater the motivation. The less ingrained and self-destructive, the less repair you will have to make with God's help.

The apostle Paul understood this turning-of-the-tables concept as the solution to his most baffling, persistent, negative behavior. His own miserably sinful tendencies were prime motivations to consistently and routinely surrender his "fleshly," destructive ways to the less immediately gratifying, yet overwhelmingly rewarding, practice of life in the Spirit, that is in Christ. Let us once again return to a passage in which, if taken out of context or left to stand on its own, the apostle easily could have been describing a substance addiction. Paul relied upon the vivid imagery of what he had been and would be apart from Christ in order to persist in his relationship with God. This is evident in his use of the present tense in his description of an absolute powerlessness for doing what is right when relying upon his own power or ability. He described it this way:

> For I have the desire to do what is good, but I cannot carry it out. For what I do is not the good I want to do; no, the evil I do not want to do—this I keep on doing. Now if I do what I do not want to do, it is no longer I who do it, but it is sin living in me that does it.   (Rom. 7:18–20)

Sin is described here as though it were a disease independently working its will. From the beginning, the Bible has alluded to the addictive nature of sin. Only recently have the behavioral sciences understood the extent to which this is true. Because we choose sin until it controls us, and each person has his or her own particular areas of predisposition to various self-destructive behavior, denial is relentless in the sinner, and sin is baffling to the person who earnestly wants to do good.

There are some things to keep in mind as you continue. Behavioral and spiritual language will sometimes be used interchangeably. Psychological explanations will be made at various points in this material. Remember, however, that this is not a study of the mind or of human nature, and you do not have to *understand* any of what little psychobabble it may contain. Do not analyze. Do what is suggested and keep it simple. And don't hesitate to turn frequently to Spirituality at a Glance. That's what it's there for.

There is a reason why Jesus requires childlike faith (Matt. 11:25). When you were a child, you were not asked by those who were responsible for you to obey only the rules that you understood or that you *felt* like obeying. Also, it was not until you reached the perspective of experience and maturity that you truly understood the importance of such things as a balanced diet or cautiously looking both ways before you crossed the street. So it is with this program. Lest you have forgotten, making it through childhood is no **Don't be** easy task. Neither is practicing childlike- **overwhelmed.** ness; yet, it is so simple, even a child can do it. Don't be overwhelmed. As a child you were not given all the rules at one time, nor were you expected to follow any of them without occasionally failing to meet their requirements. Likewise, embark on your spiritual journey one step at a time. When you fall—and you will—get back on your feet and know that God and His people will be with you every step of the way (Ezra 9:8–9).

It may seem contradictory to pound away at the notion that, rather than to intellectualize, you are to concentrate on doing what *The Promises* call for, while at the same time focusing on the nature of sin or addressing the psychology of human nature. On top of that, you are told you don't have to understand what you read. You don't have to understand, and you probably won't understand some of it by merely reading it. However, with time, both understanding and internalization will come with the practice of your new way of life. The focus of *The Promises* is not on understanding concepts. It is on applying sound biblical principles and realizing joy and miracles in your life as a result.

Why Settle for Happiness?

If you could make one broad reality happen for your children, what would it be? It would be for them to find happiness, right? You would like for them to have a good education, a comfortable income, and certainly good health. But the bottom line is that you want them to be happy. After all, you want for them only what you want for yourself. Wrong. Could it be that the search for happiness is really not your ultimate quest? However, if it really is your goal in life, allow me to direct you to the fast track. First of all, falling in love will make you happy if your love is returned. Also, making lots of money can make you happy, until you start worrying about how to hold on to that money or how to make lots more of it. A positive sexual experience will do the trick, and for an initial **Happiness is** bargain price, there are a number of substances that offer pure elation on demand. **like a flash in** Of course, the problem with sex and substances is that their happiness is like **the pan.** a flash in the pan. Besides, we human beings tend to build up tolerance toward most happiness-provoking agents.

You might have thought that happiness is the bottom line in life, and you were willing to go to any length to get it and to hang on to it. Happiness is actually relatively easy to obtain, but it can just as easily be lost. That is because happiness is basically our positive response to that which happens to us or within us. As circumstances change, so does our level of happiness. If you think happiness is hard to find because of its elusive quality, it's probably because what you have really been looking for is *joy.* The difference

Joy is born out of a person's personal relationship with God. between the secular experience of happiness and the spiritual experience of joy is far more than semantic. Rather than being the result of circumstances, joy is born out of a person's personal relationship with God. While in some cases circumstances may be falling apart, the active participant in such a relationship will experience ongoing joy. If you are looking for happiness, well, I just told you how to get it. But if you are looking for joy, roll up your sleeves, because there's lots of work to be done.

By the way, with this program you get a guarantee. If at any point you decide that this biblical spirituality is, for any reason, not for you, you can easily return to your current spiritual and emotional condition, no questions asked.

Know Your Miracles

We clarified words like *sin, living problems,* and *denial.* Before we get to the good stuff, bear with this study just a little bit longer as we clarify the terms *in the flesh, in Christ, in the Spirit,* and *miracles.* Your patience will be well rewarded.

If you are living *in the flesh,* happiness is about the best you can expect to have. Lasting joy, on the other hand, is reserved only for those *in Christ* or *in the Spirit.* *Flesh* was used as a code word by the apostle Paul to refer to the whole person living on his or her own power or direction apart from God. The Greek word is *sarx.* It is usually translated as "flesh" in the King James Version and "sinful nature" in the *New International Version* of the Bible. (See Romans 8:3, 5, 8, 9, 12, 13. Note that these are examples from only one chapter of one book.) A life *in Christ* or *in the Spirit* is one that is joyous and abundant in a healthy relationship with God. When referring to the nature of God, the terms *Christ* and *Spirit* are distinct. But when referring to our relationship with God, they may be used interchangeably. It may be noted that the body is never in and of itself referred to in the Bible as sinful. In fact, the word *body* is used frequently to refer to organized, cooperative, and supportive believers (the body of Christ). For our purposes we will use the terms *in the flesh,* and *in Christ* or *in the Spirit* to refer to two opposite qualities of existence.

Joy and miracles go hand in hand, producing a healthy cycle of living, the quality of which will exceed your wildest expectations. The miracles resulting from the practice of *The Promises* may include the substantive, but are not primarily tangible or physical in nature.

If you are to recognize the miracles that God will produce along the way of your spiritual pilgrimage, you must know what constitutes a miracle. Anyone would recognize the parting of a great body of water or the blind seeing as examples of miracles. Perhaps you prayed for someone's healing and witnessed it coming to pass. But a lasting change in someone's ingrained dysfunctional or self-destructive behavior is one of the rarest miracles of all. No less miraculous than the lame walking is the rageaholic coming under control and staying that way or the overeater eating healthily and continuing to do so. A miracle is a controlling sweetheart or spouse being empowered to "let go" to the point that intimacy and freedom in the relationship are possible. A miracle is a fragmented, dysfunctional family bonding with and enjoying one another for the first time. A miracle is an ADHD child experiencing concentration in the classroom. One of the joys of this development of spirituality is learning to appreciate miracles for what they are.

Chapter 3
Things You Need to Do

Have you done it? Have you identified your living problems? What a simple assignment, especially considering that you are undertaking an eternal spiritual process. Provided you are serious and committed, you have all the time in the world. Take it easy, and don't be afraid to unearth problems you did not know you have. Remember, they will be there whether you identify them or not. Hidden issues will only frustrate your spiritual growth, and they will impact those who are most important to you. *The Promises* will show how to commandeer them to your advantage and minimize or eliminate them altogether.

The Promises were the first thing you read following the preface. Perhaps you have reviewed them several times. At this point, you may be thinking, "Enough already! *The Promises* will do this! *The Promises* will do that! For goodness' sake, let's do 'em!" Actually, that's the spirit! Take it easy, take it one step at a time, but don't take it lying down.

The following suggestions are not merely preliminary preparations for your voyage. Like coming to grips with your living problems, these three suggestions may be fully implemented only as you aspire to *The Promises* themselves. At some point, however, they must be addressed.

First, focus on behavior, behavior, behavior. As you seek out the troubles in your life, focus on the behavior that needs to be changed. Avoid rationalizing. Whether it is a one-time or a chronic behavior, if it has caused you or others harm, stay clear of any rationale or justification of your wrongs. You will address these problems with a radical, biblically prescribed course of action. Scientific research proves what biblical faith has taught all along. If

Scientific research proves what biblical faith has taught all along.

you consistently change your behavior for the better, your attitude, and indeed your entire point of reference, will follow. There is substantial evidence that even brain chemistry adjusts accordingly. The alternatives are: attempt an easier way that will fail and reinforce your denial, or stick to the familiar, what you have always done, in which case you will be assured to get the very results you would like to change. Not good alternatives, are they?

Second, seek out and participate in a spiritual Christian fellowship. This requirement may be tough if you are a church dropout or if you have never really been exposed to church life. People who do not participate in organized religion, for whatever reason, rarely state a problem they have with God as an excuse for their boycott. After all, they usually worship a god of their own making, anyway. Such people usually target God's people as their excuse. No more excuses.

There is a strange agreement among Christians and non-Christians alike about the role the organized church plays in an individual's relationship with God. "Going to church doesn't save you" is the cliché. This statement is usually an introduction to the Christian's point that salvation is the result of God's grace, as opposed to human work or accomplishments (Eph. 2:8–9). But for many who claim to be Christians, it is part of a shallow and flawed argument that our eternal standing as "heirs of the kingdom" is unrelated to our daily behaviors. When non-Christians make this statement, it may be in the context of arguing that faith is a private matter. Both beliefs are off-base. A life that is in rebellion against God does not have God's gift of eternal life (James 2:26). Also, becoming a Christian means taking one's place as a functional member in the body of Christ. (See 1 Corinthians 12:12–31.) This point is a dark cloud over salvation for the unchurched. Don't let personal hang-ups or prejudices toward God's people separate you from God. Initiating fellowship with Christians may be your first act of intentional humility.

Speaking of humility, don't let the "h" word frighten you. This program will open up a radically new and wonderful experience of humility to you. As you systematically apply God's principles of the Beatitudes to every aspect of your day, you will come to know humility as the first and most basic of the steps in your spiritual pilgrimage. You will witness its power to transform mundane activities into redeeming victories. It will be your strong suit when you are not sure about the rules of the game. It will keep you anchored when you would be tossed about; and when all else fails, it will become a familiar source of strength. You have all this to look forward to. Follow these preparatory suggestions, and you may begin to experience it sooner rather than later.

If you are already associated with a spiritual Christian fellowship, you have a decisive advantage. A spiritual fellowship is one that focuses on relationships. A humble, intimate relationship with Jesus Christ must be the foundation of your spirituality; and healthy, trusting, and loyal relationships should characterize the body of the believers with whom you choose to align. This quality of fellowship is quite different from that found in many churches that are primarily training grounds for so-called biblical doctrine or those that focus on miracles or emotions for their own sakes. Neither doctrine, miracles, nor self-edifying feelings should be ends in themselves. They should be the results, not the focus or foundation upon which your fellowship with God and others is built.

Christian fellowship is vital for several reasons. For one, as was just mentioned, a Christian is by definition an integral working part of the body of Christ. (See 1 Corinthians 12:12–31.) Another important reason is that divine intervention and personal spirituality are wed where believers fellowship (Matt. 18:20). As a fellowship of believers, we empower each other to change our behav-

We do the work, and He provides the results. iors until many of our most chronic, seemingly hopeless problems are solved. God provides the principles in His Word. Together we do the work, and He provides the results. Voilà, the miracle of spiritual wholeness! (See Galatians 5:16–26; 6:7–10; Philippians 4:8; Hebrews 10:36.)

A third issue is the absolute necessity for accountability (James 5:16). We all create God in our own images. In our small universes, He always understands us and is on our side, while our bitter enemies have similar feelings regarding their own personal "Higher Power." That is why this program is not about helping you discover your own "Higher Power." Rather, it is about making and maintaining contact with *the* Higher Power. Accountability, which guards against our persistent tendency toward idolatry while facilitating intimacy with the one true God, is a function of both the body of believers and the personal confidant. An explanation of the functions of the personal confidant and how to obtain one will be explained in the next chapter.

Remember, isolation is the guardian of denial. Do not let the requirement of community frighten you. As was stated earlier, if you already have the support of a healthy fellowship, you have a precious advantage. We all embark upon our spiritual pilgrimages with baggage of secrets, multiple faces, and loneliness. This baggage oppresses us when we are alone, but sometimes it is worse when we are in a crowd. This program is designed to ease even the most timid sojourner into a truly spiritual fellowship of support, strength, and hope. The results will be nothing short of joyous miracles that will give glory to God. (See Psalm 143:10; Luke 11:28; John 14:15.)

Explaining the Unexplainable

A few pages back when you read the list of example living problems, did any of them describe your condition? Perhaps you were able to be more specific or identify a condition that is not mentioned. If you were asked to explain why you behave in the obsessive or compulsive way that constitutes your living problems, would you be able to? If, in keeping with denial, it is a behavior you defend, you may have a well-thought-out rationale you use, not only to convince others, but to convince yourself as well. But if you have come to the conclusion that the behavior in question must be stopped, it is very possible that you haven't the faintest idea why you keep doing it. For example, people who "shop 'til they drop" may explain that they find it relaxing or that it relieves tension. They may claim that their shopping is a lengthy, involved process because they are particular. But if it becomes obvious that excessive shopping must come to a halt because of creditors and debt, yet they are unable to do so, it is likely that they will be unable to explain why they can't just stop.

Robert Downey, Jr., and Daryl Strawberry are unable to explain why they continue to sacrifice their relationships, health, and careers for a mind-altering substance. Few will die for their faith, but an addict will sacrifice everything for a fix. Insane? Most definitely. But this kind of insanity is not restricted to substance abusers. A woman permanently scars the very children she believes she would die for by divorcing the children's father because he is either unwilling or unable to meet her self-centered craving for attention. The woman's differences with her husband become "irreconcilable." A man will sacrifice the well-being of his family in order to accomplish a vocational dream, with the conviction that he is doing it for the very people he is harming through neglect. The workaholic is convinced that someday his family will understand that much of what they are resentful over "couldn't be helped" and was "for their benefit."

You may be wondering how it can be claimed that divorce or workaholism are systems of attachment or addiction. If you are honestly and fearlessly searching out your own living problems, as you address them with this program of ego deflation, the relationship will become all too clear. Singular transgressions are very rare in human behavior. Through the practice of God's principles, you will discover that most of your discomfort or misery is related to an addiction. More important, you will discover that your new behavior will minimize or completely remove both the problems and the ill feelings your additions create.

Sin is chaotic and confusing. As difficult as you may find the addiction model of sin to accept, you will find it very compatible with the steps of the Beatitudes; and in your doing them, much of the mystery about the chronic nature of sin in your life will be solved.

A Second Case Study

Secular anthropologists claim that a primary characteristic separating humans from the rest of the animal kingdom is morality. Human beings are the only moral creatures on the earth. Romans 3:23 states, *"All have sinned and fall short of the glory of God."* Few people would argue with at least the first part of that verse. Even reprobates feel guilt for wrongdoing, provided they are not too far gone. But while guilt is intuitive, if not self-evident, the concept of sin as addiction is not. There are at least three reasons why you must be persuaded of the addictive nature of sin. First, there is denial, a theme of this chapter. Second, sin usually gains a foothold gradually. In doing so, it creates a need in its host. Third, sin just plain works. The gratification it provides is so immediate that it gives the illusion that it is a controllable agent, when in fact it is gradually taking control from its user. It is understandable that one would not be naturally inclined to choose delayed

Sin just plain works.

gratification when the attachment to an object, thought, idea, goal, substance, or person induces an immediate sense of satisfaction, counterfeit and dangerous though it may be.

A confusing but very important aspect of sin as addiction is that there is a seemingly endless list of symptomatic expressions of sin. Predispositions toward specific sins vary from person to person. A compulsive liar may accompany a friend to a gambling casino and not be tempted in the least to gamble. His friend, on the other hand, may find it completely out of character to either lie or exaggerate, yet he struggles under the burden of self-inflicted debt because of his addition to gambling. This, of course, is an illustration. Most of us support multiple addictions. A compulsive gambler may also be a compulsive liar, the cycle of which started with a need to lie in order to support his gambling. He may also routinely overextend himself financially in areas of his life beyond the influence of gambling because the chemical process in his brain created by living on the edge financially is comparable to the process that motivates him to gamble. Despite the commonality of multiple addictions, for the purpose of practicing *The Promises*, you will be fine concentrating on one addiction at a time. So let the one that causes you and others the most discomfort be your focus.

When physicians ask you if heart disease or cancer run in your family, they are trying to determine whether you have a physical predisposition to be at risk for one of those diseases. Also, your family medical history helps in diagnosis. Without the proper diagnosis, effective medical treatment is simply not possible. The moral self-examination advocated in this program is no less important to your spiritual condition, which affects your relationship to God.

Harry and Jill's Story

Harry and Jill are just plain folks. They have been faithfully married for twenty-three years; they have three children, the youngest a freshman in college; they both work outside the home; and they are never delinquent in paying their bills. They are active in their church and have a large circle of friends. They get along well with everyone, including relatives and in-laws. In the best sense of the term, they are *unusual* individuals. No one would dream that they are sufferers of active addictions.

When Jill is bored, angry, lonely, or tired, she doesn't take it out on Harry, the children, or anyone else. She eats. She, like the other women in her family, has always been overweight. She has a heavy frame for her height. She also shares the tendency for high cholesterol and high blood pressure with other women in her family. Her mother died from complications associated with diabetes. Jill is at the early stages of the disease but is still able to control her blood sugar through her diet. But she has a history of failure with strict dietary regimentation, and she has learned to cope somewhat with the depression of her "inevitable" life track by accepting that this is just the way God made her.

Harry has not been particularly supportive of Jill's many diet ventures, but he has been supportive of her as a person. It might even be said that he has been rather nurturing as husbands go. He has paid lip service to her diet campaigns, but Harry loves the taste of food as much as Jill does. When sexual intimacy was lacking in their relationship, the intimacy of breaking bread, lots of bread, filled the void. A glaring difference between Harry and Jill, and a source of contention, is that Harry's fine dining and junk food sprees never make him fat. Except for a trace of a spare tire, for a middle-aged man he is downright skinny. Jill is genetically predisposed to be overweight. Harry is genetically predisposed to be thin.

Where does morality fit in this picture? Despite the appearance that Harry eats a lot, he really does not. He loves the taste of food, but he knows when enough is enough. He does not like that full feeling, and whether his schedule dictates that he eats small amounts often or a more substantial amount twice a day, he does not obsess about food, and he does not use food as a coping mechanism.

Jill, on the other hand, as far back as she can remember, found "comfort" in food. Perhaps her mother relied on it as a primary means of quieting her child, although many mothers do that without their children becoming addicted to food. The reason, how it happened, or who's to blame is not important, and dwelling on these issues is counterproductive. What is important, as to who Jill has become, is that her chemical makeup, both physical and mental, seems to be conducive to a reliance upon the experience of eating and the sensation of being full in order to have a sense of wholeness. Food is good. Using it as Jill does is evil. In her case, it feeds, supports, and maintains the sinful nature. Jill, who suffers from hypertension and the early stages of diabetes, has the ravages to her body to prove it. Paul said, *"For when we were controlled by the sinful nature, the sinful passions aroused by the law were at work in our bodies, so that we bore fruit for death"* (Rom. 7:5).

Being a fine, church-going Christian woman, Jill refuses to believe that either her behavior or her condition is symptomatic of a spiritual problem. The notion that food occupies the God-shaped space at the core of her being would be nonsense to her. As she sees it, everyone has a burden to bear, and hers happens to be her imperfect body. She is in denial. As Jill joins her many overweight Christian friends in food-centered fellowship, she effectively keeps the core of her living problem secret, even from herself.

Harry's problem is more pronounced and therefore more difficult to keep secret than Jill's. Harry's living problem, partly because of its bizarre nature, will open the floodgate of blessings for both him and Jill, if he is in enough emotional pain to do something about it. Harry has difficulty getting into bed at night—not going to bed or falling asleep once he gets there. He has to get into bed a certain way. He is not sure how to describe the way exactly. He knows only when the way feels right, and until that sense of satisfaction and assurance is certain, he struggles getting in and out of bed with extraordinary anxiety. Sometimes it takes him twenty minutes to get into bed properly. Sometimes it takes him all night, in which case he faces the next morning stressed, without sleep, and totally exhausted.

The point has already been made that all of us suffer insanity in the form of denial, rationalization, and determination to maintain our negative behaviors while expecting different results. In the way the word *insanity* is normally used, however, referring to neurosis or psychosis, Harry is as sane as anyone. He knows that something is dreadfully wrong with his thinking process, and at times he thinks he must be nuts. But when it comes to distinguishing between what is real and what is not, Harry is, if anything, above average. His judgment is sound, he is reasonable, and there is something attractive about his "even keel" personality. Why, then, is he stricken with such uncontrollable, bizarre behavior; and more important, what can be done about it?

Harry suffers from obsessive-compulsive disorder (OCD). It is called by some the "doubting disease." In simplest terms, it is caused by irregular or low serotonin in the brain preventing information grasped by the frontal lobe to be satisfactorily transmitted to the most primitive part of the brain, the basal ganglia. The person with OCD usually obsesses and acts compulsively with regard to a particular activity. The most common OCD symptoms are excessive hand-washing, checking, ruminating, and hoarding. An individual will usually have several symptoms, but occasionally a person may exhibit almost all of them or only one. Most people can identify with the OCD experience. Have you ever pulled out of your driveway wondering if you locked the door to your house? Of course you locked it. You always do. But this time you are on your way to the airport. You will be gone for three days.

You don't have extra time. You are cutting it close, but you must go back and check the door to be sure. That is what OCD is like, although someone with the condition may check for ten or fifteen minutes, knowing full well that it is locked, yet not feeling okay about it.

There are medications for OCD. There are also medications for compulsive eating. Experts agree that when cases like these, and most disorders, are severe and chronic, the most effective and thorough treatment involves medication and spiritual or psychological guidance or therapy. Jill has tried diet clubs. She doesn't believe in taking pills for weight loss. She attended an Overeaters Anonymous (OA) meeting, but when she discovered that it was a twelve-step spiritual program, she falsely assumed that it might compete with her substantial church involvement, so she didn't go back. She will continue to diet occasionally, but she no longer seeks help and has pretty much accepted her physical condition as is.

Jill and Harry have an exceptionally good relationship under the circumstances, despite the fact that Harry's OCD has made it necessary for him and Jill to have separate bedrooms. But Harry's loss of sleep is taking its toll. In his younger days it was bad enough to put in a full day of work following a sleepless night. As people in twelve-step recovery would say, he's "sick 'n tired of being sick 'n tired." He's going to do something about it. He's going to ask his pastor to recommend a Christian counselor to help him deal with "job stress." He doesn't want his pastor to think he's a nut, and he is being honest that he is stressed out at work.

Words cannot describe the relief Harry feels when he discovers that his strange behavior has a name, that at least two percent of the population has OCD, and that there are effective treatments for his condition. His counselor explains that severe cases usually require medication. For that he would be referred to a psychiatrist. Nevertheless, medication or not, the counselor introduces Harry to *The Promises*. He presents Harry with three choices. He can work *The Promises* with medication, he can dive into them without medication at first, or he can continue in the endless cycle of his miserable state. There are, of course, other choices, but not with this counselor. Harry is highly motivated. He is going to go with just *The Promises*, at least at first. He can do this. He believes that the Bible offers practical guidelines for living. Perhaps most important, OCD has beaten him into submission. He is willing to do whatever *The Promises* require.

As has already been mentioned, OCD is caused by a chemical imbalance in the brain, but in many cases persistent right behavior can effect healing. OCD, like many disorders, including eating disorders, is by its very nature self-centered. For the sufferer of OCD, the endless, self-propelling cycle of rituals provides temporary, counterfeit relief. The dubious satisfaction of repetitive behavior fills, in a most uncomfortable and exhausting way, that God-shaped space at the core of the sufferer's being.

As Harry practices *The Promises,* and in doing so develops an understanding of them, he offers them to Jill. She is reluctant at first. After all, as she sees it, he has a chemical imbalance while her problem is the norm for a large segment of the population in a society and culture of abundance. However, as time reveals miracles in bits and pieces of her husband's life, especially when she is able to comfortably have him back in their bed for the first time in years, she wants to partake of this newfound joy. With the help of a counselor and a confidant of their choosing, each works *The Promises* at his or her own pace. They encourage one another, but they are careful to focus on their own programs while staying clear of the spiritual business and progress of the other.

What freedom and serenity they gain by relinquishing control of their disorders, of one another, and of all the other things they cannot control! They are released from the overwhelming pressure of trying to play God. Of course, they had no idea that's what they were doing, but now they know that all they have to do in order to experience unconditional joy is to concentrate on their own behaviors, doing "the next right thing," as they approach a stream of relatively simple choices one day at a time. Harry and Jill will not outgrow this program. They will graduate only when they enter eternal joy in heaven. On this earth there is no cure for sin. There is no cure for addiction. There is only the redemption of God's grace. Harry's OCD and Jill's overeating will wait patiently to resurface the moment either chooses to wander from the safe boundaries of their relationship with God. But recovery, reconciliation, and redemption are more than enough to keep them centered in unconditional joy, and it all began when they mustered the motivation to address their problems by "letting go and letting God."

What's your problem?

Chapter 4
The Attitude of Gratitude

You will like this chapter. After concentrating on your living problems, the *attitude of gratitude* will be a piece of cake. The placement of this chapter is like having your dessert first. The chapter does invite serious thought. But the attitude of gratitude contains little to struggle with, the instructions are very specific and easy to follow, and if you follow the instructions, you may catch a glimpse of joy immediately. A seven-course meal, if devoured quickly, can produce heartburn and discomfort. If it is patiently enjoyed one course at a time, that meal becomes an experience to remember. God wants your spiritual pilgrimage to be a joyful, eternal banquet. Whether you think of the *attitude of gratitude* as a very digestible appetizer or dessert, this chapter provides the next tier of preparation for *The Promises* because it is important that you approach the Beatitudes with the attitude of gratitude.

Caution: like everything else in this program that you are asked to do, just do it, and don't get bogged down in trying to understand it. As for the heavy stuff, more will sink in than you may realize. You should still be in the process of identifying your *living problems*. That's enough of a challenge for now. In this chapter, just do the simple exercise and enjoy the results.

Introducing Gratitude

The principles of the Christian life are set forth throughout God's Word. They are perhaps most distilled in the Sermon on the Mount, and particularly in the Beatitudes (Matt. 5–7; 5:3–10). However, one of the clearest examples of the straightforwardness, practicality, obtainability, and measurability of God's principles is found in the simple practice of the attitude of gratitude described as a two-step exercise in Paul's first letter to the Thessalonians.

The apostle Paul was in constant danger of persecution and death. He wrote to the Christians at Thessalonica to encourage them, as they, too, faced the worst life had to offer. He began the conclusion of his first letter to them with the following instructions: *"Be joyful always; pray continually; give thanks in all circumstances, for this is God's will for you in Christ Jesus"* (1 Thess. 5:16–18).

God wants you to be joyful. If this chapter provided these instructions without identifying them as a direct quote from Scripture, you might dismiss them as being unrealistic or just plain ridiculous. God wants you to be joyful regardless of the hand, good or bad, life has dealt you. Sound remotely sensible? But these are real instructions from a real person given to real people in a real bad situation. Knowing that we are dealing with Scripture, we have a tendency to treat this passage as containing what we think of as typical biblical ideals. While we are not sure how literally it is to be taken, or even exactly what it means, it sounds good and in some sense provides us with some sort of perfect standard.

Actually, Paul provided us with a simple, practical formula for obtaining that deep-down sense of well-being we all desire. Paul practiced this formula himself. Paul was living proof of what he spoke. Volumes have been written about the topics of joy, prayer, and gratitude. Most of us confuse the joy that is born out of a person's personal relationship with God with the elusive sensation of happiness. To *"pray without ceasing"* (1 Thess. 5:17 KJV) seems unrealistic. And to *"give thanks in all circumstances"* (v. 18) is tantamount to being outright dishonest. Even if these misconceptions are corrected with the proper study, the fact is, even the seasoned Christian often trudges forward with a daily emptiness, not unlike the carnal person. This doesn't have to be. Paul provided a simple solution to this unappealing picture by stating that it is *"God's will for you"* to *"be joyful always"* by merely praying on a continuous basis, with the purpose of your prayers being to *"give thanks in all circumstances."*

Note that Paul did not suggest that the Thessalonians "be happy always." As was elaborated upon in the previous chapter, joy and happiness are two different things. Joy is to be the norm for the Christian, and Paul provided the Thessalonians and us with a two-step routine whereby it is possible. The following is a simple exercise offering you an opportunity to learn firsthand how determined, persistent prayer, with an open-ended gratitude list as its primary substance, will result in God's gift of unconditional joy.

The Exercise of Gratitude

1. During the course of each day, establish four brief prayer periods in addition to your usual mealtime prayers. These four prayer times are to be used only for the purpose of giving thanks to God. Your prayer times should eventually include asking God for knowledge of His will for you and the ability to carry it out, and intercessory prayers for others. These additional elements are every bit as important as thanksgiving, but, following Paul's advice, begin developing your new prayer life with the foundation of gratitude. The first prayer period in the morning, before the routine of the day begins, and the last prayer period, just before bedtime, are to last

approximately ten minutes each. The midmorning and afternoon prayer times should last no longer than five minutes each. Already you have something for which to be thankful. How generous it is of God to return, for a mere thirty minutes of spiritual focus, the gift of ongoing joy.

2. You will need a spiral notebook or a journal in which to record your gratitude list. It should be at least one-half inch in thickness. If you are persistent and searching, your book will fill up fast. Until the attitude of gratitude becomes entrenched in your daily routine, it is important that you keep a written record of your progress in the practice of thanksgiving. There is something spiritually therapeutic, both in seeing our gratitude in black and white, and in the act of making the list itself. Also, it is best to use ink to discourage erasures. Your gratitude list is for your eyes only. A casual mistake may be enlightening as you revisit your list in the future.

3. Once you have your pen and paper, dive in immediately. Place the date at the top of the page, skip a line, record the time, and start listing. Write in a single column, in order to leave ample space to the right of the page for comments or observations about your gratitudes, either now or later. The time reference will be all you need to identify whether a specific list was recorded during a morning or evening ten-minute session or one of your brief reflections during the day.

4. When you first awake, before any demands are made on your time, even before you are thinking clearly, identify in your mind for whom or what you are thankful. Your mental list does not have to be lengthy. Only one thing may come to mind, like the start of a weekend, a recent accomplishment of a family member, or the privilege of experiencing an

uninterrupted night's sleep. By the time you get out of bed, you will be ready to write. Between pondering your written word and giving thanks to God, ten minutes will pass quickly. You will be ready to start your day. Midmorning, at your convenience, on the next line, mark your time at the left of the page, and directly under your morning list continue your list or repeat previous gratitudes that are already listed in the above section of the page. Referring to your list, give thanks to your heavenly Father, and move on into the day. Repeat the same exercise during early afternoon. The last activity before you go to bed should be your gratitude time. Replace any stresses of the day with your list and prayers of gratitude. At least during the first few months of your new routine, let gratitude, the seeking of God's will, and petitions of blessings for others be the only contents of your prayers. At first, such self-imposed restrictions will be difficult, especially if, like most of us, your prayers primarily amount to a wish list or bargaining with God. In addition to gratitude, your prayers will soon include requests for knowledge of God's will for you, and petitions for others. But for now, focus on gratitude.

5. At the outset of your second week of thanksgiving, you will need to make the difficult transition to giving thanks *"in all circumstances."* This involves expressing gratitude for situations that deep down inside repulse you. You don't have to mean it; you just have to do it. As dishonest as this may seem, it is a very important step in truly developing an attitude of gratitude that supports unconditional joy. One result will be a sincere appreciation for the wisdom of God's will in your life. Consider the following example: when alcoholics are restored to sobriety as the result of practicing spiritual principles, they often refer to themselves as "grateful alcoholics." By this they are giving thanks for more than restoration to sobriety and sanity. They are actually

expressing gratitude that they *are* alcoholics. They are convinced that the fragility of their alcoholic condition helps to keep them close to God. Furthermore, most recovered alcoholics would describe their spiritual condition as a matter of life or death. They take it that seriously. With that in mind, isn't the spiritual condition of all of us a matter of eternal life or eternal death?

6. A final consideration—carefully choose a Christian support group and a personal confidant. Obtaining these resources may take time and will take courage. Be open-minded in seeking a group of people whom you can trust and with whom you choose to develop spiritual quality relationships. A Sunday school class, an in-home Bible study, or a recovery group may fit the bill. If you are unable to locate such a group, you may want to start one. (See Guidelines for Building a Promise Group, pp. 204–206). Whether you avail yourself of such a resource early on or not, this book is designed to give you careful guidance that will help sustain your spiritual progress. It will also serve as a text for any group structured around *The Promises*. As for a personal confidant, a pastor, counselor, or close friend may be the person you choose to trust with your most personal thoughts. That person should, however, have the ability to reciprocate the sharing, while being somewhat emotionally detached. In most cases, this quality would exclude a family member from being the ultimate confidant. It is even better if your confidant is also practicing this spiritual exercise of gratitude. The bottom line is that *accountability* is a fundamental part of any spiritual pursuit.

As you can see, this exercise is simple to follow. At first you will wonder how long this experiment will take before you begin to receive continuous joy. For some it is immediate, but for most it is gradual. After six months you may wean yourself from the written part of the experiment. However, this is not a program from which you graduate. Joy remains constant only to the extent that you rigorously and consistently *"give thanks in all circumstances"* (1 Thess. 5:18). The lapse or termination of your practice of gratitude will, in an instant, land you squarely in the conduct of your old behavior, with its accompanying frame of mind. The fact is, you *will* neglect your attitude of gratitude at times. However, unlike the old self, you will now know that you have a choice. Even the knowledge of the choice, itself, sparks an occasion for gratitude. Thus, once again, you are on your way in the continuous prayer of the attitude of gratitude.

Are you surprised that the attitude of gratitude is so simple? Well, profundity usually is. And though it may be simple, it won't be easy. Old habits die hard, and years of a narcissistic frame of reference solidify them. Like any worthwhile pursuit, even that of pleasure, the attitude of gratitude takes work and time. Like any aspect of spirituality, it works only if you work it; and if you work it, unconditional joy will result.

Though it may be simple, it won't be easy.

You may not maintain this strict regimen of gratitude over the long haul, but your goal should be to intentionally develop an attitude of gratitude in the way you approach life in general, including the way you approach *The Promises*. Like *The Promises*, the attitude of gratitude is not a technique. It is a consistent, intentional recognition of reality. Jesus said, *"You will know the truth, and the truth will set you free"* (John 8:32). Brainwashed people do not know that they are brainwashed, but they are in bondage nevertheless. The attitude of gratitude and *The Promises* not only reveal the truth, but they free us with the capacity to know the Truth intimately.

When you practice the attitude of gratitude, you are conducting a reality check. You have heard it said that "perception is reality." Well, only reality is reality. Perception fosters misunderstanding, fear, anger, envy, and a host of other unhealthy emotions. It thrives on a manipulation of the truth, and it justifies suspicion, which is the opposite of trust. The attitude of gratitude and *The Promises,* to an even greater extent, reveal what is real, and reality is the divine anecdote for the counterproductive and destructive feelings that swirl around with secrets in our closets. If the Christian life is the straight and narrow, the attitude of gratitude leads us out of confusion and on to the right track (Matt. 7:13–14).

Part Two
D-DAY

(Just Do It!)

Chapter 5
The Promises

This is it! These are the principles you will eventually use to conduct every aspect of your life. Because each principle builds upon the previous principle, it will be necessary for you to work them in consecutive order. It will be equally necessary to work them gradually, one day at a time. Remember, it has taken you this long to become the person you are, good or bad. The miraculous changes these principles promise, not the least of which is an abiding state of joy, will likely be gradual as well. At times you may wonder if a change is actually taking place. In some cases, others may recognize the positive change in your life before you do, but persistence will be well rewarded. You will never graduate from these steps, and at no point will you practice them perfectly. Each step is designed to encourage you even when you fail. However, if at any point you decide to wash your hands of these principles or simply neglect their practice, you will return to your old self and habits swiftly. In other words, like any kind or quality of life, the Christian life requires regular and consistent maintenance.

This and remaining chapters will attempt to explain *The Promises* and related issues, although it is like trying to explain something like self-confidence to someone who has none. When you experience *The Promises* with the attitude of gratitude by doing what they require, you will know in whom and what you believe. You may not understand them, any more than you understand God's miracles or great paradoxes of truth. Yet, through the eyes of faith, these principles will make perfectly good sense. Long before you reach the sixth or seventh Promise, you will experience a new, and perhaps unfamiliar, sense of well-being. Obsessions, compulsions, or addictions will begin to loosen their

Anxieties and fears will disappear. hold. Anxieties and fears will disappear. Hopelessness will be a thing of the past, and its memory will only engender gratitude and thanksgiving. *The Promises* are designed to enable you to face all obstacles to your well-being realistically, thus further empowering you to break through denial and conquer isolation. As a result, you will experience the freedom to receive and give love, affection, and support of fellow believers every step both from and to the way.

About The Promises

In the Beatitudes, Jesus describes the eight steps of the Christian life. Lost in the poetic beauty of the various translations, some commentary is necessary for us to hear what Jesus' followers heard in the Sermon on the Mount. When Jesus said, for example, *"Blessed are the poor in spirit"* (Matt. 5:3 NKJV), being *"poor in spirit"* was a concept with which His listeners were familiar. At the same time He promised that those who practiced this particular quality of life would have joy as its parallel. *The Promises* simply translate the Beatitudes to their original meaning and implications. The first seven of the eight Beatitudes describe the actions we must take as Christians. The eighth Beatitude describes likely consequences for those of us who are, to the best of our abilities, trying to practice the first seven. Even persecution, as the result of the Christian life, cannot rob us of joy, as is reflected in the final sentence of *The Promises*.

In his classic, *The Sermon on the Mount*, Dr. Clarence Jordan describes the Beatitudes as the "stair steps" to the kingdom. The kingdom of God is God's place of absolute authority in our lives. The Beatitudes, then, are the various levels or stages of the Christian life toward which we are to strive. This centrality of the Beatitudes stands in sharp contrast to the reality that many "Bible-believing, churchgoing" Christians haven't a clue as to their meaning or even their importance. They're simply beautiful, non-rhyming verses suitable for engraving on a wall plaque or religious card. In actuality, the Beatitudes form the basis for the Sermon on the Mount. They describe the levels and content of what it means to be in Christ. The remainder of the Sermon, which is its bulk, is primarily examples of how the principles of the Beatitudes define our behavior in a series of life applications.

In the chapters that follow, the Beatitudes will be dealt with separately, as well as in their relation to each other and in their context in the Sermon on the Mount as a whole. However, before you read the Beatitudes in the form of *The Promises*, briefly consider the structure of the individual Beatitudes and how they are linked together. Also consider why they are called *Promises* and why "blessed" is translated in this work as *joy*.

In each Beatitude, a behavior or spiritual condition is stated followed by the result. The initial result of each Beatitude is *blessedness*. However, each Beatitude has an additional result stated after the spiritual condition or behavior that is unique to that particular Beatitude. For example, *"the poor in spirit"* and *"those who mourn"* are both *"blessed,"* but the specific result of being *"poor in spirit"* is *"the kingdom of heaven,"* while the result unique to *"those who mourn"* is that *"they shall be comforted."* The *"poor in spirit"* are mentioned before *"those who mourn"* because each Beatitude refers to a specific level of Christian growth. In other words, your spirituality will have to take on the quality of being *"poor in spirit"* before you will be capable of being one of *"those who mourn."* (See Matthew 5:3–4). Sound confusing? Doing what is called for in each Promise will help with clarification.

Remember, each one of these spiritual levels of living brings joy. In fact, this is why the Beatitudes are interpreted as *The Promises*. If Jesus said that living a certain way or practicing a particular behavior will result in joy, that is a promise because Jesus' word is always an absolute guarantee. Dr. Robert Schuller cleverly refers to the Beatitudes as "The Happy Attitudes." Some translations actually read, "Happy are the poor in spirit, for theirs is the kingdom of heaven." While it may be argued that both the words *blessed* and *happy* are accurate, the word *blessed* tends to be rather general or unspecific, while the word *happy* is likely to be misunderstood. The distinction between *happiness* and *joy* has already been addressed. In the interest of being precise in constructing *The Promises*, the word *joy* accurately identifies an ongoing spiritual state, which is not directly altered by human conditions, circumstances, or events. Joy, unlike its emotional counterpart happiness, is *unconditional*. Now that these distinctions have been made, let's move on to "where the action is."

To refresh your memory, let us review *The Promises* verbatim, as they appeared on pages 16–17. Note how each expresses a level of the Christian life in the purity of spiritual behavior.

❧❧❧❧❧❧❧❧❧❧❧❧❧❧❧❧❧❧❧❧❧❧

Our Lord and Savior Jesus Christ promises that we will experience divine joy, which is His will for us, to the extent that we take the following steps (Matt. 5:3–10):

1. We have joy admitting that we are powerless over sin, believing that only God can rescue and protect us, and *humbling* ourselves in all matters, trusting that, because of Him, ours is eternal life (Matt. 5:3).

2. We have joy *courageously evaluating our moral condition*, honestly admitting our immorality to

God, facing it ourselves, and confessing it to another human being, trusting that we will experience an ongoing sense of well-being (Matt. 5:4).

3. We have joy *persevering* in the present, and seeking God's will and His power to accomplish it, trusting Him, rather than ourselves, for the results (Matt. 5:5).

4. We have joy doing whatever is necessary to *make amends*, in righting any wrong we have done to others, provided it is in their best interest, with no regard to any wrong they may have done to us, trusting that God will reward us with a deep sense of satisfaction (Matt. 5:6).

5. We have joy demonstrating *compassion* to all, knowing that even at our best, we, too, are in need of it, as we trust in God for His mercy (Matt. 5:7).

6. We have joy allowing our wills to be aligned with His to the point that our *motives are pure*, trusting that we will see God's active participation in our actions (Matt. 5:8).

7. We have joy pursuing *peace* and accepting *serenity* as the result of these steps, trusting that the Prince of Peace will declare us heirs of the kingdom (Matt. 5:9).

Our Lord promises that the practice of these principles will insure our joy in the midst of even the worst possible circumstances, for ours is eternal, abundant life (Matt. 5:10–12).

૰ૺૺ૰ૺૺ૰ૺૺ૰ૺૺ૰ૺૺ૰ૺૺ૰ૺૺ૰ૺૺ૰ૺૺ૰ૺૺ૰ૺ

As mentioned earlier, there are eight Beatitudes and only seven Promises. The reason for this has already been mentioned and will be developed further in the final chapter. Here, suffice it to say that the first seven Beatitudes describe the steps we are to take along the path of the Christian life. The eighth Beatitude describes a likely consequence of our faithful practice of the first seven. This last Beatitude is addressed in the concluding sentence of *The Promises* as listed above.

A Third Case Study

In chapter 1, Frank provided our first case study of what might bring a person to the crossroads of spirituality. His openness and transparency are common among those who discover that their personal history is both a generous resource in the maintenance of their present spirituality and one of their greatest assets in helping others. Frank's story is told from his personal experience and perspective. Our second case study and this one, our third, about Rachel, are presented from the more objective third-person perspective in which the problems are more specific and obvious, but the solutions are the same.

As was true of Harry and Jill, and anyone who puts these principles into practice, both Frank and Rachel applied *The Promises* in the form of seven steps of action or practices of behavior. Each step was addressed as a separate, gradual project, although, as they progressed through the steps, previous steps were practiced simultaneously as building blocks for the subsequent step. There is no timetable for progression by which success is to be measured. Before progressing to the next step, both Frank and Rachel struggled with the first Promise dealing with humility and admitting powerlessness. At year's end, Rachel was ascending the fourth step while Frank, at that point, was practicing all seven Promises simultaneously. Each faced different problems with different backgrounds and coping skills, but both applied the same solutions at their own pace with miraculous results.

Rachel's Story

Rachel and Roy were an exceptionally attractive couple in their early thirties. They were as attractive in personality as in appearance. Of course, they had their problems. In fact, each had a glaring problem neither could ignore. Rachel was a rageaholic, and Roy was codependent. Roy's supervisor, at the end of his rope, called his squadron's chaplain. Roy was one of the squadron's sharpest junior NCOs (non-commissioned officer), with excellent career potential. But the previous night marked the third time Rachel had locked Roy out of their house in the wee hours, requiring the intervention of the base security police. This time Roy's orders were clear: "Either do something about your raving maniac of a wife once and for all or face serious disciplinary action that will bring an end to your military career." Twice during their ten years of marriage Roy had initiated divorce proceedings, only to back down as a result of sincere expressions of remorse from Rachel, framed by her earnest promises to do something about her insane anger and jealousy. She would get help, and for a while she would get better, but her suppressed rage would build to the point that her next episode would erupt more violently than before. With Roy's chain of command backing him, this time divorce appeared to be inevitable.

Roy visited an attorney, while Rachel landed in the chaplain's office primarily for support in facing the music. Rachel was right where she needed to be, not just in location, but in her overall spiritual and emotional condition. This proud, spunky, controlling, one-time debutante had been brought to her knees. This time the losses were imminent of the two things she valued most: her marriage, sick though it was, and her affiliation with the Air Force. Rachel's father was a retired Air Force psychiatrist. The Base Exchange, Commissary, base housing, hospitals, recreation centers, and schools provided the only environment and culture she had ever known. As for Roy, she was certain that she would be hard-pressed to find another companion who would allow her as many strikes at bat.

Rachel was a seasoned counselee of psychotherapy. Her psychiatrist father had availed her of a variety of counselors, approaches, and medication. There were many diagnoses of her problem. The most plausible clinical explanation was that she was addicted to the brain chemistry of her episodic rage. Her spiritual problem, an aspect that had never before been addressed, was that the empowerment, a perverted sense of control, and a fragile sense of security for a fear-laced ego provided a dependable, though sick, filler for her empty spiritual space. Rachel's father was also a practicing rageaholic.

Rachel explained to the chaplain that she had tried everything and was convinced that she was a hopeless case. She was certainly shocked when the chaplain looked at her with an insensitive smile and said, "Sounds like you've got an ironclad reason for despair...or...you're ready to admit that you are powerless over your rage and all that goes with it. You have a choice! If you choose despair, I'll be glad to let you use me as a sounding board, and you can have what's left in this box of Kleenex to take with you. But if you're willing to do whatever it takes to solve your problem, I can help. Are you ready to do anything?" With repeated nods through tears and a drenched tissue, Rachel blubbered, "I'll do anything!"

Rachel was ready, and most important, she was willing. The chaplain immediately started her on the first Promise as described in chapter 6. He required that she enroll in Sunday school and attend his Sunday morning worship service because she had no religious affiliation. She was also required to go to weekly evening meetings with other counselees who were applying the solutions of *The Promises* to their own varied problems. Respecting the wisdom of twelve-step recovery in insisting on same-sex sponsorship, the chaplain introduced Rachel to a woman who agreed to serve as her confidant. Another novel requirement was the chaplain's insistence that Rachel take her naturally obsessive focus off her marriage and apply her energy to the practice of *The Promises*. She was not to make hollow promises to Roy. She was not to attempt to make Roy change his mind about the divorce. And she was not to try to make him love her, or to make him do, think, or be anything. Despite overpowering urges to the contrary, she was to treat Roy with the same courtesy and respect she would extend to a stranger.

The first week marked as many failures as there were days, but in the weeks that followed, Rachel's slips into her old behavior became less predictable and less frequent. She never missed Sunday school, worship, meetings, or counseling, and the phone was a constant lifeline to her newfound friend and confidant.

One of the most frustrating things about Rachel's new way of living was that the more she detached from her unhealthy behavior toward Roy, the more he would press her familiar buttons. It naturally seemed unfair to Rachel that she was supposed to live by self-imposed, narrow, and sometimes humiliating principles, while Roy was free to operate according to the old familiar and "natural" rules. Despite the baffling nature of Rachel's predicament and a share of setbacks in her behavior, her counselor, group, and confidant applauded the persistence with which she applied the principles of the Beatitudes. At the outset, applying them one day at a time was not enough. At times she hung on one hour at a time or one minute or one second at a time. But those seconds, minutes, hours, and days became weeks and eventually months.

To make a long story short, Rachel discovered that her new way of living worked, and Roy discovered that the old way, at least where he and Rachel were concerned, did not. At the sixth-month point, the details to complete the divorce were put on hold. Fortunately, Roy came to believe that perhaps Rachel was becoming a new person. The ideal scenario would have been for Roy to explore his own codependent contributions to their unhealthy relationship, but that was not to be, at least not for a while. What did happen was that Roy, with no prodding or manipulation from Rachel, initiated giving the marriage another try. Approximately a year after Rachel's first appearance in the chaplain's office, she and Roy moved to a new assignment. The chaplain also received orders for a new assignment, and every couple of years he would receive a three-way conference call from Rachel and Roy in which Rachel would describe current examples of *unconditional joy* and Roy would express his profound gratitude for the miracle of their marriage.

Twelve Steps, Ten Commandments, or Seven Principles

People in twelve-step recovery have been known to jokingly remark, "God gave 'normal' people Ten Commandments. He gave us Twelve Steps." In other words, "We need more guidelines and stricter boundaries than other folk." The intention of the humorous, self-defacing statement is to make a point. A "religious" Twelve-Stepper would not normally refer to the Commandments and Steps as being an either/or proposition. The Ten Commandments are divine rules, while the Twelve Steps are referred to in the Big Book of *Alcoholics Anonymous* (page 59) as suggestions for recovering from alcoholism. Other twelve-step programs are just as specific to their singular purpose. As was mentioned in chapter 2, the Beatitudes, on the other hand, are designed to address the full range of life's living problems. The Beatitudes are to the New Testament what the Ten Commandments are to the Old.

The similarities between the Ten Commandments and the Beatitudes include: (1) they were both given directly from their Author (Exod. 20:1; Matt. 5:2); (2) both were given to chosen individuals with whom the laws and principles would be associated (Exod. 19:20; Matt. 5:1–2); (3) these called individuals would be instrumental in passing along these revelations to a divinely formed community of faith (Exod. 19:25; James 2:5); (4) both lists address the basic issues of relationships, with God first and then with one another (Exod. 20:2–17; Matt. 5:3–10); (5) both are given and received in an elevated place, a mountain (Exod. 19:20; Matt. 5:1); and (6) neither is designed to compete with or replace the other (Matt. 5:17–20; 22:36–40).

They are dissimilar in that: (1) the former contains ten while the latter totals eight (summarizing seven actual action principles); and (2) as seekers of God's will, one list basically catalogs what we must do and not do, while the other describes qualities of actions that constitute various levels and stages of spiritual development.

As for their practical applications, the Ten Commandments are basic, eternal, foundational rules and the Beatitudes are principles for living that, by design, defy the human tendency to manipulate, rationalize, or find loopholes. God's laws are straightforward and plain to anyone who has not developed spiritual numbness. The wisdom of the Beatitudes, on the other hand, is revealed only as one puts them into practice. One of the apostle Paul's major themes was the law's purpose of defining and making us aware of our guilt (Rom. 2:12). The law makes it clear that our only hope is God's grace through our Lord Jesus Christ. (See Galatians 2:21; 5:4.) *The Promises* define our active participation in God's gift of grace as we experience the abundant life of unconditional joy, "in the eternal now."

Most people believe that there is a God, but most people do not believe in (trust) God. Likewise, most people follow divinely inspired basic tenets of right and wrong, but most people have no concept, much less experience, of living by *The Promises*. By choosing *The Promises* as your modus operandi, you should be aware at the outset not to expect others to play by the rules that you have chosen. You are not responsible for the actions of others. You are only responsible for your own. By now it should be clear that you are to relinquish control of your universe to God. *The Promises* show you how to do this. Focusing on your own behavior to do the right thing will free you from the disappointments of expectations and the resentments they cause. You will be amazed at the pure power and pleasure you will derive from your new "live and let live" policy. Your new way of living will literally be a paradox in motion. By not wasting valu- **You are to** able energy on the impossible, like trying **relinquish** to control others, you may very well wit- **control to God.** ness positive changes from the people who need it most.

To be sure, you will always be tempted to fall back into the old ways, to play by the old rules, and when the situation seems warranted, to "fight fire with fire." But you will increasingly resist those temptations, and you will be encouraged by the sheer joy of experiencing a better way to live. You will no longer find it necessary to fight with anyone or anything, and you will be free from the exasperating impossible duty of playing God.

Thus you have three complementary, rather than competing, resources undergirding the abundant life God has planned for you: Twelve Steps, Ten Commandments, and seven principles. If you have an overwhelming, debilitating addiction, it is hoped that the humility characteristic of this program will provide inspiration and courage to seek that special help and support that only twelve-step recovery can provide. The Ten Commandments are simply God's standard for human behavior. Anything less is "missing the mark."

People in recovery have a weird but refreshing way of remembering the insanity of their addiction. They say it beat them into submission, and then they met their self-destruction with the victory of willingness. The Commandments inspire us with the knowledge of our depravity. Our self-made conditions are unacceptable to God. When we meet that understanding with willingness to change, we are ready to take certain steps that will lead us with a childlike anticipation to the Christmas Tree of Life adorned with the priceless gifts of grace, mercy, forgiveness, justification, reconciliation, and all the other indescribable holy gifts that have their reality in personal experience.

On Your Mark, Get Set, Go!

People who do the warm-up exercises, such as identifying living problems and establishing the attitude of gratitude, discover that they are well on their way before the starting shot is fired. Some people, however, are unable to get into it until, well, until they get into it. Nevertheless, whether you think of it as a warm-up lap or getting yourself into the proper position for maximum speed coming out of the gate, there is one final exercise before the event itself that you are encouraged to do at least once a day, every day: recite *The Promises,* including the opening and closing sentences. It will only be a matter of days before you will be able to recite them in your sleep. Do this simple exercise, and then just do the steps one at a time.

If you are a perfectionist, there's a living problem right there. Jesus said in the very sermon that contained the Beatitudes, *"Be perfect, therefore, as your heavenly Father is perfect"* (Matt. 5:48). This He called for in the context of loving your enemies. He also said in the same sermon, *"Unless your righteousness surpasses that of the Pharisees and the teachers of the law, you will certainly not enter the kingdom of heaven"* (v. 20). The Pharisees and teachers were perfectionists when it came to following every jot and tittle of the law. But like all perfectionists, theirs were simply self-centered human preferences. They were inflexible when it came to reaching beyond what was familiar or seemed safe. If you approach this program as a perfectionist, you will be setting yourself up for failure. You'll have the "perfect" excuse for not working the program at all. The fact that you cannot do it exactly right or perfectly should serve as a reminder of why you need these practical guidelines in the first place. Beware up front of the dangers of unhealthy pride in perfectionism. Rest assured that if you chose the faith of willingness, God will work miracles in you, and often they will materialize

God will work miracles in you.

in spite of you. So get out of the way, let go, and let God have His wonderful way with you.

Thus, here is another one of those paradoxes. Relax, take it easy, don't fight with anyone or anything, "live and let live," and "let go and let God." And now, *on your mark, get set, GO!* (See Philippians 3:12–14.)

Chapter 6
Humbling Ourselves

Blessed are the poor in spirit,
for theirs is the kingdom of heaven.
—Matthew 5:3

Our Lord and Savior Jesus Christ promises that we will experience divine joy, which is His will for us, to the extent that we take the following steps:

1. We have joy admitting that we are powerless over sin, believing that only God can rescue and protect us, and *humbling* ourselves in all matters, trusting that, because of Him, ours is eternal life.

This is where life in Christ begins. This first step is the one you took, or at least intended to take, when you opened up your heart inviting Jesus into your life as Savior and Lord. Of course, if you have not received Jesus Christ as your Lord and Savior, this step will serve as a thorough invitation. Brace yourself as you experience the *power* in powerlessness. You will come to appreciate the value of your problems, self-generated or otherwise, in fostering a willingness to respond to God's invitation. And you will experience the uplifting and liberating quality of humility through the practice of simple exercises that will yield a surprising sense of self-confidence, self-esteem, and unconditional joy.

A Fourth Case Study

Linda loved her husband. She loved her children. She would never intentionally do anything to hurt them. She was a physically fit, super soccer mom and loved to prove it. She even brought home some of the "bacon," and the home she brought it to was as neat as a pin, primarily due to her efforts.

Linda had every reason to be stressed, and she was—big time. But she had one extra-curricular activity that brought relief as nothing else could. Everyone needs an outlet, something they enjoy. Linda loved to shop. Her motto was "Shop 'til you drop." What would be an exhausting exercise in endurance for some, like her husband and kids, was euphoric for Linda and her three best friends. She lived for Saturday when Dad could take charge of the eight- and ten-year-old, while she plunged into her well-deserved distraction. Although Linda maintained that it was the experience of shopping, not her purchases, that brought her pleasure, stuff was mounting, she was plunging the family into debt, and her marriage was in serious trouble.

On her way to work, she heard the news report that the average American family rolls the new year over with at least several thousand dollars of credit card debt. She was no different than her three shopping companions and millions of other women (and men, too, for that matter.)

Linda's world was out of control, further driving her to the refuge of the mall. She would go there, but this time, she was determined to buy nothing. In fact, she loaded up the "shop-mobile" with odds and ends and several big ticket items to return for refunds. She would actually help the desperate situation.

Victory! Linda made her round trip and stuck to her plan. She bought nothing and returned with the refund cash to boot. And now, "the rest of the story."

Linda was able, with the help of an understanding husband, to put the pieces of her marriage, finances, and family back together. But it wasn't because of her dubious "victory" of refund cash. That visit only primed the pump of false confidence that she could control her shopping sprees. It was a combination of "hitting bottom" and her discovery of this first step, explained during a seminar on *The Promises* at her church, that turned the tide.

Linda was a "born again" Christian who had allowed the innocent act of shopping to ever-so-cunningly take charge of her spiritual core. It is in no way melodramatic to describe her first step as a willingness to submit to the surgical removal of an out-of-control cancer that was devouring, not only her life, but the lives of those she held most dear.

With the help of a confidant and several others who responded to the seminar at church, all shopping came to a halt! Under the circumstances, her husband was more than willing to endure the considerable inconvenience of taking over the entire task—groceries, paper and soap products, school supplies, and shoes for the kids—the whole nine yards.

Today Linda does shop when, and only when, there is a need. She has learned a great deal. She has learned that her shopping companions were really only fair-weather friends. She learned that her initial "withdrawals" were a small price to pay to have her life back. And she discovered that when her relationship with the Lord is on track, it takes very little to make her happy. Of course, even when she's not happy, she still has something even better—unconditional joy!

How do you admit that you are "powerless over sin"? Why would you even want to? Good questions. Very few people believe that they are powerless over sin. Most would agree that life would be boring without a little sin in their lives. Perhaps you know of someone who lives a painful existence of avoiding every imaginable temptation. Such an individual only confirms the hollowness of fanaticism. On the surface it may appear that this first step calls for a rather obsessive avoidance of temptation, but in reality, this step offers freedom from obsessions and anxieties.

When you admit that you are "powerless over sin," you acknowledge that sin is so powerfully dangerous that you simply cannot flirt with it and go unscathed. You don't play with it, fight it, manipulate it, or run from it. You leave it alone, and if circumstances require, with self-control and confidence you remove it (Matt. 5:29–30).

The recovered alcoholic serves as an excellent illustration of how this works. A curse to alcoholics is the delusion that with enough determination they can drink responsibly. The paramount change in their lives comes when they, for whatever reason, realize that it is that first drink that gets them drunk. That is all it takes to set another spree in motion. At some point the recovered alcoholic accepted the reality that for her or him, abstinence from alcohol is the only option. Most people would agree that drunkenness, if for no other reason than its pure destructiveness, is a sin. Some Christian traditions reject the use of alcohol altogether. As strange as it may seem, however, this is not the position of most recovered alcoholics. They see the substance of alcohol as neither good nor evil. They neither encourage nor discourage its use. They applaud the heavy drinker who is able to give it up on his own power. They are neither threatened by nor resentful toward the moderate drinker. They do not even avoid social gatherings where alcohol is served if they are confident that there is a good reason for their being there. They simply know that under no circumstances will they drink, try, or taste an alcoholic beverage. They feel comfortable with their soda or coffee in hand, and they do not draw attention to themselves as martyrs or as models of behavior.

> Experience the power in powerlessness.

At the outset of the alcoholic's recovery, he took drastic measures. He was assured by fellow alcoholics who understood his disease that anything less than complete honesty and total commitment would assure failure. He might have entered treatment, but at the very least, he probably attended meetings every day. He became grateful that his god of the bottle, the slow killer to which he had devoted himself entirely, had beaten him into the submission of the spiritual program of Alcoholics Anonymous. As he matured in sobriety, he became comfortable living "one day at a time."

If asked by a skeptic from his past if he thought he could "stay on the wagon," he might shock them with the reply, "I may get drunk tomorrow, but not today. Today I'll call my sponsor (confidant), read my Big Book, and go to a meeting." Recovered alcoholics thrive on helping alcoholics who still suffer. They develop the most intimate friendships imaginable. And, in an atmosphere of laughter and gratitude, they inspire others with the gory details of their pasts and how they found relief. In this description, if the word *alcohol* were substituted with the word *sin*, the Big Book with the Bible, and the fellowship of AA with the body of Christ, you would have an outline of what the Christian life should be. As was described in "The Mustread Preface," alcoholics learned this stuff from Christians during the 1930s, while Christians were moving onto "grander" things. Is it possible that the pure basics of Christianity are unfamiliar, radical enigmas to even seasoned professors of the faith today?

If you are armed with the knowledge of your living problems, like the alcoholic, overeater, or compulsive gambler, you are now ready to admit that you are powerless over sin. Let's look, therefore, at this step more closely.

Powerlessness, Trust, and Humility

Like all *The Promises*, the first one is stated from our vantage point. Jesus said, *"Blessed are the poor in spirit."* If we take this all-important first step, then we are *"the poor in spirit"* to whom He was referring. Note, the reference is to our collective joy. "We (not I) have joy." This is a significant distinction because today's role model is often a Lone Ranger. Not so in the first century. People have always been selfish and self-centered, but the people in Palestine during the first century, like people of most cultures throughout history, saw themselves as a rather minute part of a large ebb and flow of existence. A primary concern of a member of the masses was to find and maintain his or her place in this larger-than-life world. Jesus offered an answer to this concern and could effectively address the crowd that followed Him with the same individual effectiveness that the constant reference to "you" is intended to accomplish in this book.

In Luke 6:20–26, in what is often referred to as the Sermon on the Plain, Jesus looks specifically at His disciples and says, *"Blessed are you who are poor, for yours is the kingdom of God"* (v. 20). Here He is speaking to a much smaller group than the "crowds" who followed Him primarily out of curiosity, but He still addresses His disciples as a group. The point is that spirituality does not occur in isolation, even if there are only two or more gathered in His name (Matt. 18:20). To be sure, just as was the case with Jesus, your spirituality will require that you separate from others, perhaps on a regular basis, to attend to your personal relationship with God. However, the born-again believer is never alone, **Spirituality doesn't occur in isolation.** and because of your relationship with God, as a new creation in Christ, a significant portion of your nature involves your place and function in the body of Christ. (See Ephesians 4:1–16.)

If your religious background is that of evangelical Christianity, you have certainly been exposed to the passionate focus upon your personal relationship with Jesus Christ. Your willingness to take your place in the body of Christ is of crucial importance, as well. It is at this point that many stumble. Rarely does an unbeliever reject God based on what he or she believes, or even feels, about God. The unbeliever's rejection is usually that of his or her perceived notion of what Christians believe or of how they behave. In other words, although the church has no saving power in and of itself, a person's persistent pride—as expressed in the rejection of the body of Christ, God's people—is a sure route to eternal punishment and death. That is why, if you are seeking the joy and abundant life that is only to be found in a healthy relationship with God, you must come to terms with where you stand in relationship with God's people. This does not mean that you *approve of* or *agree with* fellow believers regarding all their actions or issues of faith. It does mean, however, that you *accept* your fellow Christians as equals and as partners in spiritual growth and ministry. The issue is revisited here because this is a crucial step in tearing down the barrier of pride, which protects your denial and supports and maintains those areas of your life that are dysfunctional and self-destructive.

One of the most dreaded of human experiences is that of powerlessness. You have in common with all people a relentless desire and sometimes passionate struggle to control your environment and yourself. A common source of anxiety and negative stress is the inability to do this. Although you cannot control them, you can and will dramatically influence them, and in a positive way, to the extent that you exercise self-control by consciously turning the reins over to God. See, you can't avoid paradox. Actually, this fits nicely with our Lord's many other paradoxical principles, such as the last shall be first, the least shall be the greatest, those who would save their lives must be willing to lose them for Christ's sake, and the list goes on.

If you think that exercising a certain amount of control in various areas of your life is not only healthy but also fundamental to survival, you are absolutely correct. However, because sin is aggressively alive in the world, all of us seem to have a predisposition in some areas of our lives in which control issues are destined to be out of control. In many cases, these predispositions have their physical component. For example, some people can drink excessively for years and yet not become alcoholics, while others drink alcoholically and suffer from the slavery of cravings upon their initial exposure to the substance. Most people love food and sex, yet most people do not become bona fide overeaters or sex addicts. Everyone gets angry, but only a few become rageaholics. These and similar examples of out-of-control behavior originate from the human attempt to induce and control euphoria or a general sense of well-being.

Out-of-control behavior stems from the human attempt to be in control.

Each person seems to have an area of weakness that can be linked to his or her physiology or brain chemistry, whereby what might normally be a purely innocent attempt at diversion becomes a self-destructive case of the controlled becoming the controller. Early on, self-centeredness fuels the escalation of any dysfunctional, obsessive-compulsive, or addictive behavior, but eventually the self-destructive behavior will fuel the self-centeredness. Thus, a destructive cycle is established that is bafflingly alluring and protected by denial. This self-destructive cycle is self-perpetuating to the point that even the most intelligent and gifted person will rationalize its negative effects away. This baffling, self-propelling power is why sin often seems to have a life of its own.

You, like all people, have your own self-propelling cycles of sin. Depending upon the size of their orbit, some may be obviously identifiable, such as dangerous, compulsive overspending. Some may be so minute that they are almost undetectable, or they may appear to be characterized by healthy behavior, such as the person in the early stages of a codependent relationship, or an exercise fanatic who appears to be committed to his or her health. As in the case of the "health nut," the reality may be that his or her emotional and physical dependence upon the endorphins that the exercise releases prevents an otherwise perfect model of health from coping without an endorphins "fix."

No one awakens to a new day feeling on top of the world—with wonderfully secure and healthy relationships, with plenty of money, and with excellent health—and decides that, despite this fortune, he or she is going to strive to have a more personal, intimate relationship with God. No, there must be crisis. Counterfeit solutions to the human dilemma genuinely seem to be adequate at the initial stages of our dependence upon them. Most people invest quite a bit of energy pursuing someone or something to do for them in a fleeting moment what only God can do for them eternally.

If, in your case, your substitute for God has turned on you, especially to the point of bringing you to your knees, then in typical paradoxical fashion, what feels like a painfully destructive tragedy may very well be the best thing that ever happened to you. Whether your "hitting bottom" is a pink slip or a terminal diagnosis, if your experience has brought you to the point of "admitting that [you] are powerless over sin, believing that only God can rescue and protect [you]," you have reason for gratitude. You're taking that all-important first step into eternal life. Just as the poor in Jesus' day understood what it meant to be totally dependent upon their employer or master, you are experiencing a *liberating dependence* upon God.

But what if you took this step of receiving Jesus Christ as your Lord and Savior a year ago or ten years ago, and your life has not significantly improved? Maybe you did everything you were instructed to do. Perhaps you attended worship and Bible study, or even assumed a leadership role in the church's ministry. Yet here you are, depressed, angry, lonely, or any number of other spiritual or emotional conditions, to the point that you have concluded that Christians are not any better off than anyone else. To be sure, when you took that first step of willingness and commitment to follow Jesus Christ, you experienced a powerful glimpse of hope, purpose, and joy. You expected that, with time, life would get better. Yet you haven't experienced anything that even closely compares to that initial euphoria of surrendering to Christ, and life doesn't seem to be getting progressively better.

The answer to your dilemma is so simple that you are encouraged not to be ashamed that you missed it. If you look around at all the miserable Christians, you will realize that your spiritual condition is all too common. If you are not experiencing the rewards of personal spiritual growth and the unconditional joy that Jesus promises in each of the Beatitudes, it is not because God has neglected you or because your capacity to experience Him is less than it should be. It is simply that, for whatever reason, you have neglected to take this first step anew, one day at a time. Just as you never graduate from the Beatitudes, you never complete this first step once and for all.

If you are taking this step for the first time or for the first time in a long time, you may need to practice "letting go" one hour at a time, or even one minute at a time. The Beatitudes describe Christian growth at progressive levels as set forth in practical steps of behavior. Just as the attitude of gratitude is an ongoing, open-ended practice, each step becomes a continuous, growing foundation for the step at the next level. Your appreciation of this will increase as you regularly practice the first step while simultaneously progressing to step two and beyond.

Let us return now to the issue of admitting powerlessness over sin. We are all self-centered and selfish. Self-centeredness fosters sin. Sin is anything that goes against God's will, but it particularly involves our controlling attempts to fill the void within all of us through someone or something that is counterfeit. This substitute is usually obtained through a spiritual shortcut that often appears to be manipulatable. In other words, any attempt to deny God His rightful place of lordship in our lives is sin. Sin is alluring and, as has already been mentioned, appeals to our weaknesses to the point that it eventually controls us in a seemingly self-propelled process. "Admitting that we are powerless over sin" is to commit ourselves to the conviction that sin is so spiritually dangerous that it is something with which we cannot flirt. As the first Promise states, we believe "that only God can rescue and protect us" from sin and from ourselves. This spiritual realization and commitment uplifts us to the liberating point of humbling ourselves in all matters. Thus we come to the key of the first Promise or Beatitude: *humility.*

"Admitting that we are powerless over sin" is perhaps the purest form of repentance. Some evangelists and preachers seem to avoid the word *repentance.* Perhaps they feel it to be archaic, or they are afraid it might take the focus from the positive aspects of their message of faith and redemption. However, a call to repentance was at the

Sin is too dangerous to flirt with.

heart of Jesus' message as He introduced His earthly ministry. (See Matthew 4:17; Mark 1:15.) Mark recorded our Lord relying upon a simple three-point message. First, *"the kingdom of God is at hand"* (Mark 1:15 NKJV). The announcement of the kingdom of God is a call to humility. It refers to God's absolute lordship and our total dependence upon Him. The implication is that the kingdom is before you; therefore, what are you going to do with this opportunity? Are you going to reject the invitation to citizenship in the kingdom, or are you going to respond by trusting God? Jesus announces the kingdom, but He calls for repentance: *"Repent"* (v. 15 NKJV).

Maybe you've heard sermons illustrating repentance as the act of halting your journey in the fast lane to a dead end, making a hundred-and-eighty-degree turn, and going in the opposite direction of spirituality and abundant life. Once you have turned around, admitting powerlessness over sin, *"believe in the gospel"* (v. 15 NKJV), the Good News. In keeping with Jesus' first Beatitude, you are going to believe by exercising your trust in God to rescue and protect you from your typically destructive environment and self. In other words, the invitation of Jesus' lordship, the making of the hundred-and-eighty-degree turn, and absolute trust in the one true God provide a powerfully simple three-point outline that is as relevant for evangelism today as it was for Jesus' first sermons and His Beatitudes.

Genuine humility is uplifting and liberating. False humility reeks of pride, and "humble pie" is not even akin to genuine humility. Most people's concept of humility is that of a quality that naturally goes against the grain of human nature.

When contrasted with our secular society, humility is simply not marketable. Every product and activity on the market is directed toward the ego, particularly in the area of personal control. Personal computers, microwave ovens, VCRs, retirement programs, travel packages, cell phones—these products or packages are sold as diversions or as time-savers intended to provide you with more choices and give you more control over your life. Most Americans have at least some of these things, and they also seem to have less time, get bored quickly with the choices they have, and feel that they are the ones being controlled by all kinds of external and internal forces competing for their attention. Humility, on the other hand, is a direct result of admitting powerlessness, and powerlessness is the direct opposite of all this control that is for sale. Paradoxically, the more control you seek, the more likely you are to experience a lack of control, while the act of relinquishing control has the power to bring order, meaning, and security to real or perceived chaos.

Compare the modern attached or addicted personality with the historic person of Jesus. Our Lord is the ultimate example of self-emptying, while demonstrating the self-esteem of the ultimate calling. He was confident, intentional, and moved freely and comfortably in any social circle or circumstance, including those that were dangerous or life-threatening. Although He traveled by foot and His ministry kept Him constantly on the move, He always had time for what was important—people.

Of course, technically, Jesus had all power in heaven and earth; but by another miracle of paradox, He gave up His sovereignty, and by demonstrating the courage of accepting the Cross, He defeated sin once and for all. He also did exactly what He requires of us and demonstrated what is meant by admitting powerlessness over sin. He was tempted as we are, but at no point did He flirt with sin or try it out on a controlled basis. Even as He was tempted in the desert by the devil after forty days and nights of fasting, to each of the tempter's glamorous invitations of *shortcuts* to power, control, and personal comfort, He "just said no" by quoting Scripture (Matt. 4:1–11).

When you admit that you are powerless over sin, you are simply saying no to sin. "Believing that only God can rescue and protect" you from sin and death, you are exercising the choice of allowing God to help you abstain from sinful behavior, regardless of the extent to which you have previously practiced it or felt a craving to try it. The mere act of admitting to sin's power and destructiveness is an act of humility.

Avoiding sin is a very proactive activity. It includes vigilant prayer, in keeping with the Lord's Prayer, that we not be led into temptation. It liberates us from the hopeless, often subconscious, activity of "playing God." And yes, you will find the practice of humility *uplifting.* With time you will begin to understand that, despite the fact that you are insignificant in the universal scheme of things, God has taken such care to nurture His relationship with you because He obviously considers you to be that important to Him. Also, in direct contrast with conventional and popular wisdom, which attempts to foster self-esteem through self and ego edification, you will be amazed that your self-esteem will actually grow commensurate with the deflation of your ego.

Proactive Ways to Humble Yourself

Just as getting in shape physically requires that you exercise your body, developing a confidence-building, uplifting, and liberating humility requires that you routinely practice humbling, ego-deflating exercises. The following suggestions have been proven effective, but they are merely suggestions to stimulate your own creativity in discovering what works best for you. If you are currently practicing the attitude of gratitude, you are already involved in an activity that is, at the same time, humbling and joyful. In addition, consider the following suggestions:

1. Do something good for someone *anonymously.*

2. Apologize immediately and directly to anyone you may have, for any reason, offended or harmed.

3. Do something nice or charitable for someone you honestly believe doesn't deserve it. Make sure it is something he or she will appreciate.

4. Choose a habit or behavior that is irritating to someone with whom you are close or intimate, and no matter how uncomfortable or painful, do your absolute best to bring it to a halt.

If these examples seem silly or extreme, or perhaps insignificant, be assured, they are not! And do not consider their simplicity an insult to your intelligence. Remember, the goal is humility. These simple suggestions may describe actions quite different from your usual behavior. The most brilliant mind will tend to repeat behavior while expecting different results. If a golfer misses a green and the ball lands in the water, rather than repeat the shot with another club, he is likely to use the same club while hitting from the same place with the same swing while expecting the ball, this time, to reach the target.

If a wife does what her husband perceives to be nagging in an effort to get his attention, and he persists in emotionally shutting her out, rather than to take a different approach at sparking his interest, she is likely to increase the so-called nagging, thoroughly expecting that, by doing so, she will get the desired results. If problems in your life in any way involve your behavior, part of the solution is to do whatever it takes to change your behavior.

Pride expects others to change or circumstances to change. *Humility* requires that, regardless of the circumstances or actions of others, your concern is your behavior.

By the time you are well into this first step, you will begin to understand how obsessive attempts to control others or things only add to your problems, rather than helping to solve them. You will be amazed at how concentrating on doing the right thing yourself to the best of your ability will often significantly contribute to bringing order out of chaos. You will discover that humility is an extremely powerful asset. You will be able to handle what was previously unmanageable. And you will experience a sense of self-confidence, self-esteem, and freedom, which provides nothing less than unconditional joy.

Don't Wait

An additional note: don't *wait* for these miracles to happen before moving on to the next level. There is no waiting in this program. Those who try, and then step back to wait and see, are most likely to give up at the very point where the miracle is about to take place. Besides, the remaining steps are, by their very nature, a continuation of this one. Each level is, in essence, an exercise in the acceptance of reality. Your routine practice of raw honesty yields humility—yours. With the help of your confidant and anyone else you thoroughly trust, when you are convinced that you are squarely on the road to humility, you are ready to take the next step.

Chapter 7
Our Moral Condition

Blessed are those who mourn,
for they will be comforted.
—Matthew 5:4

2. We have joy *courageously evaluating our moral condition*, honestly admitting our immorality to God, facing it ourselves, and confessing it to another human being, trusting that we will experience an ongoing sense of well-being.

It has been said that digging a ditch is simple, but it is not easy. Taking a personal moral inventory is also simple, but not easy. Unlike ditch digging, however, if you are *courageously honest* in your moral "digging," this step may very well be one of the most rewarding experiences you ever have. This chapter contains guidelines for developing your inventory, warnings about the dangers of expectations and resentments, and the necessity and amazing rewards of deflating the ego.

A Fifth Case Study

Jeff had a secret. To this day, no one knows what that secret was except Jeff, his confidant, and God. Jeff met twice a week with three other guys who were working *The Promises*. They all started together, but two of them were

107

on Step Three, one was on Step Four, and Jeff was stuck on Step Two. He had followed the suggestions for developing a personal moral inventory precisely. He confessed to God, repented of every little sin he could dig up out of his rather eventful past. And he told his confidant everything—everything except his one secret.

The time came when his confidant decided enough is enough. "Jeff, ole buddy, you know I love you, but until you decide to let go of whatever this is you're hanging onto, I think these meetings (other than the ones with the group) are wasting your time and mine." Jeff looked down at the tabletop. The pause seemed as though it would have lasted forever, except for the confidant's frustrated body language. "Okay, (pause), here it is."

"That's it?!" laughed the confidant in disbelief. "You've been stuck on that?" There was nothing rude or cruel about the confidant's response. He matched Jeff's secret with one better of his own. Furthermore, his natural and easy acceptance of Jeff imparted a sense of relief and the confidence that, yes, there was one human being on earth who knew all about him and still loved and respected him.

Taking Inventory

When grieving the loss of a loved one or friend, how is it possible, at the same time, to experience joy? Actually, in the second Beatitude, Jesus was not addressing grief in the usual sense. In order to understand who and what Jesus was referring to by *"those who mourn,"* it is helpful to understand what mourning involved for Jews in the first century. When contrasted with the way technologically civilized people express grief today, you will find that we are unique from all generations and cultures before us. Human beings throughout history and in most cultures have viewed protracted outward expressions of grief as a necessary and healthy part of life.

In the first century, as throughout history, the body of the deceased was displayed in a common living area, and those closest to the deceased directly participated in preparing the body. Today, professionals at a funeral home attempt to expedite the process as quickly and as painlessly as possible. In the first century, mourning was more than a period of time that embodied the emotion of grief. It was an intentional, prescribed activity involving fellow mourners. In fact, the open display and communal aspects of the grief process were so important that those of power and means often instructed underlings to adorn the proper attire and join in the weeping and wailing. In some cases, particularly where the deceased was unpopular, wealthy survivors would hire people for the task.

As for the healthy aspects of mourning, it was a time for survivors to recognize their loss; face and internalize the realities of death and their own mortality; and take positive steps to resolve regrets, adjust to the impact of life without the deceased, and celebrate life. The spiritual mourning Jesus called for as the second level of the Christian life requires that we "courageously evaluate our moral condition, honestly admitting our immorality to God, facing it ourselves, and confessing it to another human being." Just as mourners courageously faced the loss of their loved one, so we, despite a lifetime of denial and fantasy regarding both our motives and behaviors, are to courageously face the reality of where we came from, what we have or haven't done, who we are, and how we got here.

People who grow up in a dysfunctional family do not realize that what they are familiar with is unhealthy, unless lengthy exposure to a healthy environment proves to them otherwise. At the same time, they are unlikely to be interested in or submit to a healthy environment unless their dysfunctional ways are causing them considerable discomfort or pain; and even then, as soon as the discomfort subsides, they return to that which they know and with which they feel most comfortable.

Therefore, if you are, for whatever reason, motivated to move ever closer to Christ, which is the purpose of these steps, God will rescue and keep you in an intimate relationship with Him. But you must provide the willingness to face the fear of the unfamiliar. If at any point you feel overwhelmed, remember that you cannot, nor are you expected to, digest any of this on your own or all at once. You must be empowered by God and supported by fellow Christians, and you can expect to do only what you can do one day at a time. Nor are you expected to be thrilled with the prospect of taking a thorough and honest moral inventory. Depending upon the seriousness with which it is taken, some may even find it terrifying. However, as in the first step, this moral inventory takes confidence, self-esteem, and finally, liberation to the next level. Therefore, lest the philosophizing frighten you further, dive right into this ultimately joyous experience. Here's how.

"Courageously evaluating our moral condition" requires patient and thorough self-examination. Like the development of your attitude of gratitude, this process is so important, yet unnatural, that you will want to journal your progress on paper. You may not like the sound of your voice when you play it back on a recorder, and perhaps you have been surprised, even embarrassed, to see yourself candidly on video. The fact is, none of us sees things exactly as they are, not only because we are finite, but also because we do not see ourselves as we really are.

We have a tendency to think that God sees things our way. We judge others based on their actions. But we judge ourselves based on our perceptions of our motives. Most of us have a god who is on our side. We forget that the god of those we do not like, and even of our outright enemies, is on their side, too. This natural way of thinking is prideful and is an example of why the first step must be practiced simultaneously with the other steps and with this step in particular.

Writing your inventory on paper allows you to drain off some of the emotional sludge by the sheer act of writing. It's as though some of the overflow is drained off with the ink from your pen. Oh, yes, do use ink. The written version of your moral inventory belongs only to God and you. Written mistakes of any kind may prove to be valuable when revisited to evaluate your progress of spiritual growth. Also, your written product will allow you to step back to evaluate yourself much more objectively than relying upon memory. Eventually you will want to destroy your written inventory because, if you do it thoroughly, it will contain information that might be embarrassing or hurtful if read by someone else. However, provided you store it in a safe place, you should keep it long enough to help you appreciate your spiritual, emotional, and behavioral growth. Daily improvement may be difficult to evaluate, but return to this material a year, or even six months, from now, and you will be amazed at your progress.

There is no one correct way to record your personal moral inventory. However, there are some elements that every inventory should contain.

1. The pages of your inventory should be kept in some sort of bound form, such as a diary, spiral notebook, or test booklet. This should help you keep the pages in order and discourage you from tearing out and disposing of pages containing writing you are displeased with. Also, your personal inventory may require several such volumes. It is not unusual for a thorough self-examination to exceed the fifty-page mark. Your inventory should contain a chapter chronicling accomplishments of which you are proud. Bear in mind, this is not an "immoral" inventory. One purpose of this exercise is ego deflation, but it is not intended to involve self-bashing. As was mentioned in a previous chapter, the goal is not to think less of yourself; it is to think of yourself less. It may never cease to amaze you, but if your inventory is done honestly and thoroughly, as your ego deflates, your self-esteem will rise.

2. Second, your inventory should contain a chapter of people you resent. Resentments should be addressed with the most recent ones first. As your list develops, you will want to reach as far back into your past as possible. List the person you resent on the left side of the page. Next to the person's name, in the middle of the page, briefly describe in short bullet sentences why you resent that person. Be sure to skip enough lines between entries so that you will have the necessary space to write out your explanation, but remember, these explanations are primarily to jog your memory. Therefore, complete or grammatically correct sentences are not necessary. Once you have described your resentment to your satisfaction, on the right side of the page, describe how you are affected by your resentment. Thus, your list of those you resent will consist of their names, the reasons for your resentment, and how your resentment has affected you. Your most recent entry may be a spouse or a friend, and your past resentments may extend as far back as a playmate who mistreated you in preschool. Regardless of where you are time-wise with your list, always feel free to add to your list as resentments occur. On page 65 of *Alcoholics Anonymous*, the book from which the organization took its name, there is what is referred to as "our grudge list." The following example is the list as it appears in the AA book.* Use it as your model for the second chapter of the inventory recommended here.

---

* See note at end of chapter.

I resent:	The cause:	Affects my:
Mr. Brown	His attention to my wife.	Sex relations. Self-esteem (fear).
	Told my wife of my mistress.	Sex relations. Self-esteem (fear).
	Brown may get my job at the office.	Security. Self-esteem (fear).
Mrs. Jones	She's a nut—she snubbed me. She committed her husband for drinking. He's my friend. She's a gossip.	Personal relationship. Self-esteem (fear).
My employer	Unreasonable— Unjust—Overbearing. Threatens to fire me for drinking and padding my expense account.	Self-esteem (fear). Security.
My wife	Misunderstands and nags. Likes Brown. Wants house put in her name.	Pride—Personal/ sex relations. Security (fear).

3. The third and final chapter of your personal moral inventory will require courageous honesty as well. But it may also require some imagination. You are to list any and every person who, as far back as you can remember, may have or at one time had, as far as you know, any reason to hold a resentment toward you. As with your chapter on your resentments, list his or her name on the left side of the page and a brief explanation of why he or she may or should resent you on the right. Thus, your personal moral inventory would be comprised of three chapters. The first will list your positive accomplishments, the second will list those you hold resentment toward and why, and the third will list those who hold resentment toward you and why. You may get tired of the word *resentment,* but remember, it is a powerful, destructive force with which you must deal.

Also remember that *repentance* means that you stop going down the literally dead-end street of sin and, making a hundred-and-eighty-degree turn, you begin to move forward in the newness of life. In order to repent of your sins, you must know what they are and be willing to face them squarely. Just as counselors sometimes video their clients to help them more clearly see themselves as they really are, the thorough process of compiling your transgressions and the prayerful self-searching of facing them will help you confess your sins to God, cleansing your soul in the process.

For many, confession is nothing more than a blanket recognition that since *"all have sinned"* (Rom. 3:23 NKJV), being a sinner simply means that we are only human. True confession, on the other hand, requires that we identify specific sins that we are willing to stop committing. At this point, you will hopefully see the value of practicing Step One while simultaneously working Step Two. We sin because sin works. It accomplishes, in a counterfeit way, what we want it to accomplish, when we want to accomplish it. Consequently, we behave as though sin is worth guarding—and at a heavy price. For this reason we must constantly admit "that we are powerless over sin, believing that only God can rescue and protect us." But we must also specifically recognize the sins we are powerless over.

God knows our sins whether we confess them or not, but we confess our sins to Him because we must recognize them, and because He is the only one from whom we *must* receive forgiveness. Why, then, does this second step require that we also confess our sins to another human being? According to James 5:16, the participation of our fellow believers in our process of confession is necessary because forgiveness is equated with genuine, deep-down healing. Those of us who have done it know that this may be the most difficult aspect of the second step. **Confession requires that you swallow your pride.** Like a bitter pill, it requires that you swallow your pride. But remember that pride, and the ego it protects, has such an awesome power of eternal self-destructive consequences that this should be, in and of itself, enough to motivate and inspire you to take whatever measures are necessary to turn from the spiritual cancer of an inflated ego. Such will literally eat you alive. But there is an additional reason to seek out the audience of another human being.

Since we all have a tendency to create a higher power who is on our side, our mythical deity is likely to overlook our chronic emotional game-playing. When that is the case, we are able to secure a bogus pardon with a mere recognition of "mistakes" or "inadequacies," or with a convincing "passing of the buck." Again, how many times have you heard the phrase "we all make mistakes" referring to sinful behavior? In most cases, another human being, someone in whom you have confidence and trust, would be more perceptive and straightforward than your fictitious deity.

If your confidant has a clear understanding of what you are trying to do in your spiritual quest and why you are trying to do it, he or she is more likely to hold your feet to the fire than the god of your creation. Your confidant will be in a position to facilitate accountability and generally aid and encourage you in your pursuit of the truth about yourself and the world of which you are a part. There are also benefits that cannot be adequately explained, but rather, must be experienced. They are the remarkable sensations of joy, self-confidence, and the personal satisfaction of knowing that there is a least one person in this world who knows everything about you, including your deepest, darkest secrets, yet still supports and *respects* you. Your confidant may well match your confessions with confessions of his or her own, further challenging the lies of ego, pride, and isolation.

Like many of the truly difficult pursuits in life, this one is usually considered by those who have done it to be the most rewarding part of performing this second step. Conducting this task closely with your confidant will help reinforce the reality that, while there is no one else like you in all God's creation, your transgressions, character defects, and basic spiritual needs are in no way unique. Joy, security, and satisfaction will emanate from your common experiences with your confidant and your ongoing bonding with fellow members of the body of Christ.

Expectations, Resentments, and Deflating the Ego

Expectations and resentments are dual enemies of every child of God. Unmet expectations foster disappointments and resentments. For this reason, this entire section will depart briefly from the progression of the steps to focus on these two maladies and what to do about them. Together, or by themselves, they generate divorce, violence, feuds, prejudices, and outright war. Equally tragic is that these maladies are passed along from one generation to the next. Both expectations and resentments are grounded in the deadly sin of pride, and they both result in and emanate from a false sense of self-importance characterized by an endless list of personal rights and entitlements.

While the dangers of resentments may be somewhat self-evident and commonsensical, regarding expectations you may ask the questions: Aren't certain expectations reasonable or even appropriate? Doesn't everyone have the right to expect certain things, like fidelity from a spouse, for example, or positive rewards for acts of goodness and charity, and mutual respect by virtue of our common humanity? The answer is that people *should* behave this way, but this "should" is the very seed of sabotage that diverts us from an appropriate, humble response to our environment.

"Should" is the seed of sabotage.

In a world where we are all bombarded by sin and personally contribute our fair share of it, God does not blanket humanity with certain inalienable rights. *"Yet to all who received him, to those who believed in his name, he gave the right to become children of God"* (John 1:12). *"The right"* here refers to our transformation as full-fledged members of the family of God. The analogy is one of adoption. This *"right"* is a bestowed privilege, not something to which we have a natural birthright. Only those who want to be adopted are adopted and, therefore, the message is one of God's *gift* of salvation and our response to His gift, rather than any entitlements we may intrinsically have. In 1 Corinthians 9:4–5, Paul argued for the authenticity of his apostleship by referring to *"the right"* of an apostle, but his point was that in order to serve Christ, he was willing to give up various rights. The bottom line is that you cannot focus on your "rights" and on Christ at the same time, any more than you can love both God and mammon or serve two masters (Matt. 6:24).

When you set expectations, you are employing your "rights" and exercising grandiosity. When you expect, for example, to be received with open arms by those from whom you desire acceptance, or when you expect the weather to be conducive to a planned outing, you are operating on an inflated ego.

By choosing to establish expectations, you are setting yourself up for disappointment and a resulting resentment. The greater the expectation, the greater the danger. Shattered expectations can result in the breakup of a marriage or a friendship, alienation and isolation, and a false sense of rejection or defeat. In order to be in Christ, you must "accept life on life's terms." When you do what is right in any circumstance, with no regard to your rights and with no expectations, you are likely to be pleasantly surprised.

There is an alternative to expectations. That alternative is *hope*. In the famous Love Chapter of 1 Corinthians 13, Paul said, *"And now these three remain: faith, hope and love"* (v. 13). After describing those things that would pass away, he identified these as lasting. Paul did not say "faith, *expectations*, and love." As you grow in Christ, you grow in hope. Hope provides the same capacity for planning, preparing, and setting standards of excellence that are usually associated with high expectations. But, whereas expectations are born out of self-centeredness and belief in entitlements, hope is based on promises of God and is an act of humility. When you expect, you demand. When you hope, you trust God.

When you hope, you trust God.

If expectations set you up for a fall, resentments keep you there. Resentments are the reliving of anger, conscious or otherwise, as a result of a perceived threat. The word *perceived* is used because, just as most of the things we worry about never come to fruition, so many things that we consider to be threatening are in fact no threat at all. Life is too fleeting and precious to waste a single moment of our spiritual and emotional energy on contrived enemies. In many cases, resolving resentment is the equivalent of loosening chains of bondage. If you are free of resentment, you are free indeed.

Anger, like fear, is an emotion designed for our protection. Just as practically any excess becomes destructive, so when anger turns into resentment, it becomes a cancer to our spiritual and emotional well-being. Resentments, like expectations, are self-centered and ego-driven. When you nurse resentments, you set yourself in a place of privilege where you confer value upon others based upon how they act toward and revolve around you.

Resentments make us miserable, while often those we resent go unaware. Paradoxically, resentments are difficult to shake off because they feel so right. In this respect, resentments, like other addictive agents, can take on a life of their own, and as with any attachment, they can serve as a counterfeit diversion from the pain within. They are an unhealthy way for us to focus outside ourselves, even though in reality they feed our egocentric selves.

Resentments can take on a life of their own.

Freedom from resentment is infinitely more than a highly preferred option. You may want to brace yourself for this, but it is nothing less than *essential* on your part in the process of your salvation. In fact, Jesus said, *"If you forgive men when they sin against you, your heavenly Father will also forgive you. But if you do not forgive men their sins, your Father will not forgive your sins"* (Matt. 6:14–15). Depending on your theological perspective, you may find this statement difficult to swallow, even though it is a quote from Jesus Himself.

It is interesting that some of the best, most accurate commentaries give little or no attention to the significance of these verses, not only as they stand alone, but also in their application as the only direct commentary Jesus amplified, referring to the specific request for forgiveness in His many-faceted Lord's Prayer (Matt. 6:12). In the commentaries that do address these verses, most state that our Lord was not suggesting that our acts of forgiveness cause God to forgive us or somehow obtain our forgiveness. The caution, of course, is against a "works theology." The bottom line, however, is exactly what Jesus said, as He said it. Nothing more, nothing less. And this doesn't mean that we "buy" our own forgiveness by forgiving others. Forgiveness in particular, like salvation in general, is a gift from God that all the forgiving in the world or good behavior cannot buy.

Regardless of whether you consider your forgiveness of others to be essential to your salvation, you can easily prove to yourself that it is essential to your personal relationship with God. Simply try nurturing your resentment and your relationship with God at the same time. If you are "courageously honest" with yourself, the futility and absurdity of nurturing both will be obvious.

Resentments are such a waste. Consider, for example, that your next-door neighbors allow their dog to "soil" your yard. This happens frequently, after which they call the dog in with no thought of their inconsiderateness. They think nothing of it, while you allow it to ruin your evenings. You may want to walk next door and politely ask them not to allow their dog to soil your yard. You may want to give them a scooper as a "gift." But regardless of how you handle it, you must let it go. This is an occasion to give thanks for the roof over your head and the luxury of having a lawn to care for. It is an occasion to question whether you also occasionally exhibit behavior in certain areas that others might consider disgusting or thoughtless.

You must let it go. It is not an occasion to rob you of precious time in the present. Resentments fester and grow. They lead to "irreconcilable" divorces. Churches split because of them, and some of the members use them as an excuse to turn their backs on the Christian community altogether. People carry unresolved bitterness to the grave.

While resentments have the capacity to enslave us, the most dangerous and difficult kind are those that provide a dubious pleasure, like the ones that give us a false justification for revenge. They are the ones that give us a sense of superiority, sometimes subconsciously, and in doing so, they feed our egos, which leads to the third and final focus of this section.

Have you ever asked one or both of the following straightforward questions: What is spirituality? How do I become spiritual? There is one answer to both questions, and it is as straightforward as the questions themselves. Yet it eludes people to the point that, even with years of prayer, Bible study, and Christian fellowship, some just seem to be unable to "get it." The answer to both questions is: *Deflate the ego!* Doing this is both what **Deflate** spirituality is and how it is achieved. Our Lord is waiting patiently to fill the vast, God-shaped **the ego!** space in our lives, but He will not do this while it is inhabited by a bloated, self-shaped ego.

An explanation of "deflating the ego" requires that we repeat some truths that have already been stated, perhaps in different ways. Of course, please bear in mind that much of the success in applying Christ's principles is grounded in repetition. Remember, evil brainwashing influences are repeatedly thrown at you at every turn. The following discussion of the ego and its relation to self-esteem cannot be repeated enough.

The carnal world panders to the ego. It builds it and manipulates it. This is the goal of both mindless pleasure on one end of the spectrum and much of the popular counseling and self-help techniques on the other. In the flesh, the conventional wisdom is that the route to self-esteem is through the ego. The truth is that the building up of one results in the lowering of the other. The ego and healthy self-esteem may be accurately described as direct opposites. Ego-centeredness is self-centeredness. The ego has an insatiable appetite, and egocentric people always "need" more of whatever they think it is outside of themselves that will satisfy this inferior, lonely, and fearful monster within. Egocentric people live in the dark shadow of the sometimes subconscious, but ever present, fear that they will either not get what they want or that they will lose something they have.

Being in Christ is an ongoing experience filled with self-esteem. The phrase "deflate the ego" emphasizes that the ego is, in fact, our worst enemy, and that there is no step among the Beatitudes that is too radical to minimize this persistent enemy. As the ego goes down, self-esteem goes up, provided that the ego is replaced with Christ as the center of our devotion. Fear disappears because *"if God is for us, who can be against us?"* (Rom. 8:31). In Christ, we have a sense that royalty and undeserved privilege have been bestowed upon us. The result is a self-esteem that defies description.

This is spirituality. This is the goal and purpose of the Beatitudes. Spirituality is not to be confused with New Age orgies of self-love, nor is it to be confused with many so-called mainline religious practices. For example, spirituality is not synonymous with religious or church activities. Such activities should serve as vehicles of spiritual growth, but they can also serve as busy diversions from the primary business of placing God first and dealing with relationships with God and fellow human beings. Spirituality is not emotionalism. Healthy relationships with God and others deeply impact our emotions, to be sure, but the principles elaborated on in *The Promises* are to dictate the way we conduct ourselves, rather than our emotions. People who depend upon their emotions to confirm their spirituality find themselves on a roller coaster, with God lifting them to the heights while He is nowhere to be found in the depths. Spirituality is quite different from riding the crest of a spiritual high. True spirituality is a leveling experience of consistency in all areas of one's life.

Spirituality is not synonymous with strict behavior. The yoke of our Lord and Savior is not confining and burdensome (Matt. 11:29–30). It is true that *The Promises* guide us in behavior that goes against the grain of the grasping, driven, or emotionally incapacitated person in the flesh. Nevertheless, life in Christ is one of freedom, opportunities, and joy. This is quite different from a life regulated by meticulous rules and refined doctrines commonly propagated by those who claim to have a monopoly on the truth.

Finally, there is a common misconception that many people have when attempting to discern spirituality. They equate it with being "nice." This is derived from the idea that all Christians should have similar gentle, friendly, happy personalities. In church brochures and newsletters, on revival and Christian music concert postures, on the inside flaps of Christian books, and on the covers of contemporary Christian CDs, broad, clone-like smiles convey a glow as the fundamental mark of being a Christian. Such smiles may, however, very well mask the rigid Pharisee or the performer desperate for recognition. People who are obsessed with the way they project themselves are seething with self-centeredness.

If you immerse yourself in *The Promises,* you will no doubt develop an inviting, humble quality that may also be termed as "nice." It will be marked by integrity and genuineness and may develop in your personality so gradually that others will recognize it before you do. It will be of the quality of the request made by the anonymous little girl who was credited with praying the simple prayer, "Dear God, please make the bad people good and the good people nice." Suffice it to say, Christians don't always smile, act energetic and outgoing, or emit an attractive glow. But when they do, it is genuine.

There is an additional aspect to this misconception that Christians are always "nice." Practicing the principles of the Beatitudes is an ongoing exercise in seeking and doing God's will. In doing so, you may appear to be seeking human approval because of your concern for the welfare and best interest of others. On the other hand, your persistent quest to do what is right will, at times, go against the grain of the status quo. After all, God's rules are different from those of the egocentric majority. As an obstacle of resistance, you may even incur the wrath of persecutors, like those referred to in the eight Beatitude. Doing your best to do the right thing in a given circumstance may be an exercise of "love," which may or may not be welcomed by the object of that love.

In an atmosphere of both blatant and hidden forces clamoring for your attention and devotion, being in Christ requires that you put God first; but in doing so, the needs of others will take on a new priority. Paradoxically, in the process, you will increase your capacity to be who you need to be for those who truly need you, and this is a very different dynamic than "obsessive people-pleasing."

Expectations, resentments, and deflating the ego are laced with paradox, as is so common with truth. Expectations position us for a fall. They set us up for and lead us to resentments. Expectations demand that the ego be fed, creating an appetite that only frustrates the cancerous ego in that it can never be satisfied. In other words, like an addictive substance, expectations frustrate and harm their craving host. The alternative to expectations is hope. Hope trusts God, an act that liberates the soul from the self-destructive bondage of the ego and in the process provides a satisfaction that is not dependent upon the outside forces of circumstance.

The alternative to expectations is hope.

Resentments, like expectations, declare and feed upon a factitious "divine right" of the ego. Resentments foster the kind of condemning judgment that Jesus warned about in His humorous illustration of the person with a plank in his eye focusing attention upon his neighbor whose vision is impeded by a speck of sawdust (Matt. 7:1–5). Paradoxically, our resentful judgments amplify the flaws in our moral vision and attest to the absurdity that we value people based on their relationship to us rather than their relationship to God. Resentments help no one and they hurt the resenter most of all. Expectations lead to resentments, resentments alienate us from others and separate us from God, and the solution to this tragic dilemma is the surgical removal of the wounded, inflamed ego by way of the steps of the Beatitudes.

Thus, in keeping with the paradox of truth, deflating the ego is not destructive at all. It is an absolutely necessary, ongoing housecleaning of the person in Christ. It disinfects that vast, scarred, God-shaped space in all of us that only God can fill. Commensurate with the minimizing of the ego is the maximizing of self-esteem. We work, and God provides the miracle, resulting in the fact that *"if anyone is **in Christ**, he is a **new** creation"* (2 Cor. 5:17, emphasis added).

---

*The excerpt on page 113, from *Alcoholics Anonymous*, is reprinted with permission of Alcoholics Anonymous World Services, Inc. (AAWS). Permission to reprint this excerpt does not mean that AAWS has reviewed or approved the contents of this publication, or that AAWS necessarily agrees with the views expressed herein. AA is a program of recovery from alcoholism *only*—use of these excerpts in connection with programs and activities which are patterned after AA, but which address other problems, or in any other non-AA context, does not imply otherwise. Additionally, while AA is a spiritual program, AA is not a religious program. Thus, AA is not affiliated or allied with any sect, denomination, or specific religious belief.

Chapter 8

Persevering in the Present

Blessed are the meek,
for they will inherit the earth.
—Matthew 5:5

3. We have joy *persevering* in the present, and seeking God's will and His power to accomplish it, trusting Him, rather than ourselves, for the results.

The *perseverance* aspect of this next step is one you probably have considerable experience with—perhaps more than you realize. Have you ever set a goal and followed through with whatever was necessary to reach it? Perhaps the goal was a certain level of education or training. Maybe it was to recover from a lengthy illness. Perhaps you put everything into winning a sweetheart, obtaining a certain vocation or position in an organization, or raising a child. If you can bask in the personal satisfaction of anything you would consider to be a quite an accomplishment, you are then familiar with *perseverance*.

A Sixth Case Study

Sue could not control her anger. A recently separated mother of one, she had literally scarred everyone she had ever loved with her explosive fits of rage. She had come to understand that the chemical reflex in her brain to certain triggers was as much a part of her body function as cravings are to the hard-core addict.

Sue had no religious background, but she did have a neighbor in her apartment complex who had heard her hideous, intrusive rage in the wee hours. Rather than complaining to the management as other tenants had done, she approached Sue with genuine concern and showed her a marked, well-studied pamphlet containing information about *The Promises*. Sue defensively rejected the kind woman's outreach initially, but she did accept the pamphlet.

Six months and three steps later, she found herself hovering over divorce papers, trembling at the heart-breaking finality of the procedure as she received the attorney's expensive pen. She did not want this inevitable divorce. Submitting to it was the hardest, saddest thing she had ever done.

As she turned in a fog of tears for the cold, hard marble of the foyer, the clicking of her steps seemed to jar a new reflex—one so incredibly contrary to anger and revenge. As though the clicking were in stereo, she felt the movement and company of the supporting flank of her new-found friends. Her neighbor taking her arm to her left and a Bible study partner on her right were the first two people she had not driven away. Her persistent admitting powerlessness over her rage, and trusting God to rescue and protect her; her liberating inventory that, with her neighbor's support, filled a volume and a half; her ever-so-gradual move to the present, allowing her to get up and brush herself off when she fell—all were bringing into focus her first real miracle.

Sue would see her friends that evening, and she would need their company, but she chose to drive alone to the church preschool to pick up her daughter. She did not think, she knew, her circumstances would get better because she was better, and her new life in Christ was proof. Before her transformation (very much in progress), her mind's eye would have imagined countless scenarios of revenge against her husband, and she would have despised him, but not today. Sue had been praying real prayers for him for months. She was grateful for what little time with him she had not squandered, and she was determined to make it as easy as possible for him to participate in their daughter's life.

Sue was hurt, hurt badly. But this time she knew who the real enemy was, and it was someone she could do something about.

The key ingredients for success, according to many who have achieved it, are determination, desire, and discipline. These qualities are far more important than intellect, economic resources, or physical ability. If you have immersed yourself in *The Promises* with honesty and humility, it can be nothing less than awe inspiring, and nothing can separate you from the love of God (Rom. 8:28–39). Nothing can deny you from an unconditionally joyous relationship with Him *if you want it.*

It really comes down to just that. Do you want it? It was the question you dealt with when you were challenged to count the cost. On the surface it may appear to be a no-brainer, but considering the fact that Bible-believing Christians have always been in the minority, it is obvious that God's free gift of salvation is overwhelmingly rejected. Being captain of their own fate by serving a lesser god is what people are familiar with, and most people will cling to the familiar at any cost. So the question boils down to, Do you want an intimate relationship with God enough to persevere until you have it?

Perseverance is fundamental in any important endeavor. Commenting on why some brilliant college students drop out while other good and mediocre students graduate and may continue on to graduate or professional studies, an educator put it this way: "Academic pursuits are impacted far more by endurance than intellect." Engaged couples would be shocked and amazed at how many of those couples they admire, who have been married for forty years or more, have experienced dry spells or mere survival, after which they rediscovered one another more as a result of commitment than of love. In other words, if something is important, it usually takes time, and time requires perseverance. Now here's the good news about Step Three.

When you apply perseverance to *The Promises* with a firm foothold on Steps One and Two, time equals eternity. Time is no longer your enemy, because you are living in the eternal *now*. It's one thing to persevere on your own power, fighting boredom and at times just "hanging in there." As you will see, it is quite another, joyous experience when you persevere "in the present." One of the first things many who ascend Step Three conclude is that, while they have experienced a sense of satisfaction in their own act of perseverance, they have never experienced it with joy in progress like this.

Hopefully, this chapter will provide a picturesque context for where you are at this point in your spiritual growth. It will attempt to clarify the connection between perseverance and the biblical quality of meekness. You will be alerted to the ever-lurking danger of diversions to your spiritual progress. This step will empower you to live "smarter, not harder" by helping you focus your physical, mental, and spiritual energies on what you *can* control. And, as important as any of these issues, the challenge to "trust [God], rather than ourselves, for the results" of our best behavior will be addressed.

Practicing the first two Beatitudes is hard work because they simply go against the grain of your natural inclinations to seize control or run for cover, or both. At the same time, they are invigorating and yield the attitude of gratitude. Remember, the foundation of your spiritual structure is Jesus Christ. For the sake of illustration, think of a pyramid. The ground floor is "humbling ourselves in all matters." If you internalize this humility by recognizing and demonstrating your absolute dependence upon God, you establish a base whereby you can, using God's blueprint and resources, construct the second floor of "courageously evaluating [your] moral condition." With these two floors firmly constructed and in constant repair, you are now ready to move directly to this extremely important third level, "persevering in the present."

The first and most common question is, What connection does perseverance have with the biblical quality of meekness? In the Bible, the two people described as *"meek"* are Moses in the Old Testament and Jesus in the New Testament (Num. 12:3 KJV; Matt. 11:29 KJV). Our Lord's humility was, of course, His choice. Moses had a host of frailties, yet he emerged as a towering figure in the Old Testament. These examples counter the misconception that there is some sort of link between meekness and weakness. Humility, yes; weakness, no. Nor is the meek person spiritless or "harmless." Religious leaders considered Jesus to be so much of a threat that they devoted themselves to destroying Him. Pharaoh no doubt considered Moses, as God's spokesman and conduit of authority, to be his worst nightmare. Life in Christ involves developing convictions, and convictions will always be interpreted as being threatening by some. Convictions both inspire perseverance and require it. Anticipating the controversies faithful Christians would stir up, Jesus devoted the last Beatitude and the remaining two verses that follow to the issue of the danger, yet reward, of persecution (Matt. 5:10–12). Persecution is perhaps the ultimate test of perseverance.

The link between meekness and perseverance is an important one because each fine-tunes our understanding of the other. Just as meekness is sometimes confused with weakness or a dependent, doormat personality, perseverance is often associated with an "in your face, take the bull by the horns" mentality. The fact is that neither describes the behavior or the personality of the person who is immersed in this step. To persevere, one does not focus on controlling one's circumstances or

Meekness is sometimes confused with weakness.

the actions of others. In fact, perseverance in Christ is, in and of itself, an act of relinquishing attempts to control the things that, in reality, we neither can control nor should be trying to control. Relinquishing control frees us to concentrate on what we really know deep down inside should be our own behavior. This natural, deep-down moral sense—a sense we almost instinctively struggle to overwhelm, suppress, or ignore—is our spiritual connection to the discovery of our inner desire to know God's will for us and to have the ability to accomplish it.

We can look at horses to provide another illustration of the meekness we're aiming for. Although they appear to be independent and unpredictable in the wild, they actually, like humans, possess a herd mentality. Wild horses have even been known to follow the herd into life-threatening situations. In contrast, Roy Rogers' famous horse, Trigger, was a tame, gentle, and humble animal—a paragon of meekness. As horses go, he was extremely intelligent and powerful. He answered only to Roy, and under his master's control, the two worked as one. By relinquishing control of our reins to God, we can learn this kind of meekness.

Perseverance is not simply getting up each time you fall. It's also not just staying on the course of right action. Perseverance involves consistency within the self-imposed boundaries of the Beatitudes. Apart from this context, one could conceivably persevere in all sorts of meandering, meaningless, and hopeless directions. This consistent adherence to the principles in these steps is absolutely necessary for "letting go and letting God," which is the essence of spirituality. "Letting go and letting God" seems too simple to capture the prism of spirituality. However, it is, at the same time, one of the most difficult tasks we will ever undertake. Second only to the Lord's Prayer, the Serenity Prayer is perhaps the most trusted and utilized resource for ardent sojourners of spirituality. Just as the Lord's Prayer addresses head-on the issue of Christ-centered control versus self-centered control in its petition

"Thy kingdom come. Thy will be done" (Matt. 6:10 KJV), so the short form of the Serenity Prayer is both a plea for God's assistance in this matter and a defining reminder of what this matter involves.

Serenity Prayer

God grant me the Serenity
To accept the things I cannot change,
Courage to change the things I can,
And Wisdom to know the difference.

In gift shops, flea markets, and Christian bookstores, the Serenity Prayer adorns plaques, plates, pictures, and parchment. Like the Beatitudes and the Ten Commandments, the Serenity Prayer sounds great and looks great. It is so profound, yet so simple to recite; and its message is so focused, yet few people have a clue as to its meaning. Its practical value is such that the topics of *serenity, acceptance, change, courage,* and *wisdom* would serve you well as separate studies in your spiritual pilgrimage. Here, however, we think that the various components of the Serenity Prayer are best understood first and foremost through the experience of practice. In other words, it is suggested that you pray the Serenity Prayer faithfully and often as an aid and encouragement to perseverance, so that by the time you develop your own personal study of the prayer's content, your understanding will have been shaped by your spiritual practice rather than having your spiritual practice shaped by your understanding. At this point, in order to get to the heart of the prayer, note that when it comes to discerning between those things that you can change and those that you cannot, the only thing or person solidly in the realm of your control is *you.*

If part of persevering is getting up each time you fall, doing it in the present is equally important, straightforward, and simple. At the same time, while persevering is difficult to do, living in the present is also difficult to do—and for some it is even difficult to grasp. It should be obvious to anyone that we can neither change the past nor be guaranteed a certain future. Yet most people spend so much time reliving the past, either as "the good old days" or in the form of resentments, or they dread or eagerly anticipate the future, that the divine experience of the present, by and large, sifts through their fingers.

This sense of wasting precious moments is a root source of much of the suppressed guilt and widespread anxiety that permeates every level of the current social fabric. This anxiety, in turn, stimulates a ruminating of the past and/or dread of the future. Guilt is once again produced, thus completing a self-destructive, self-induced, and self-generating cycle. This self-perpetuating cycle is most commonly manifested as *addiction* or *attachment,* whether in symptomatic behavior or as a dubious coping diversion. This is one reason why an understanding of addiction provides excellent insight into the biblical concept of sin in its most comprehensive sense.

Sin and addiction are not synonyms, as the biblical writers certainly had no concept of the medical or physiological model of brain chemistry or function. However, just as there are numerous distinctions in the Bible between individual sins and sin as a state of being, so we distinguish between a potentially addictive act and the disease of addiction. The solidifying quality of attachments, their entrenched addictive nature, is further complicated by the natural human inclination to employ diversion as perhaps the most common and widespread coping technique.

Diversion

There is nothing unhealthy about diversion in and of itself. As a matter of fact, while ruminating about the past or future becomes a subconscious form of diversion for some, diversion activities themselves are often acts of focus on the present, down to the moment. For example, when you are involved in an athletic activity, if you are to execute a move properly, you will automatically think with split-second awareness. Just as attachments are self-reinforcing, so are healthy, active pursuits in that, while they focus us on the moment, they also provide the release of endorphins, thus stimulating a sense of well-being. It is no wonder that when people proclaim themselves to be "addicted" to golf, tennis, running, or some other challenging physical activity, they are right on target.

The careful examination of the dynamics of diversion is important, because they are natural and healthy as coping mechanisms, while at the same time they can derail spiritual progress by providing a counterfeit version of that sense of well-being that only God can adequately provide. Practically every mental and emotional path of diversion is forked with the accessible and attractive expressways leading to a dead-end of dependence that feels familiar and comfortable, yet has the capacity to isolate, obstruct, and enslave.

Be aware that the most innocent diversion can escalate to a full-blown addiction, provided you are predisposed for it to do so. Often you cannot be certain of such a predisposition until it is too late. Couch potatoes with TV remotes in hand, "shop 'til you drop" weekend warriors, fans who *must* have their sports, and family providers who spend so much time providing that there are only occasional flashes of so-called quality time with the family, all demonstrate both the power of denial and the devotion with which we cling to our coping mechanisms. Living in the past or future robs us of the divine reality that is found only in the present, but when diversions are taken to excess, they simply ignore or bypass the divine moment altogether. To put it simply, you cannot experience the profound joy of oneness with God at the same time you are nursing a diversion from reality.

Spirituality is ego-deflating. Diversions are generally ego-inflating. They provide us with the sensation of being out of ourselves, but from the vantage point of self-centered control. Whether the perversion of diversion is a substance or activities like shoplifting, obsessive work, or even obsessive religious ritual, you might say a diversion provides a fleeting sense of euphoria or well-being on demand. Despite the passive, detached, milk-toast "higher power" marketed today, the Bible teaches that the heavenly Father is a jealous God who created us for Himself. God will not compete with or be replaced by a diversion, nor will He serve as a diversion. He requires nothing short of an intimate relationship, and that's what is necessary for us to genuinely experience joy and freedom. By contrast, as subtle and as gradual as some diversions may be, they provide inconsistent moments of pleasure with the capacity to enslave us. In the face of the relentless temptation to become dependent on our many diversions, the divine empowerment of "persevering in the present" is that crucial third step we must take early on in our spiritual pilgrimages.

> **God will not compete with diversions.**

Unhealthy diversions are primarily activities or thought processes that we either choose or naturally gravitate toward in order to shield ourselves from pain or discomfort. This pain may either be encountered or simply perceived to exist in the present. Our avoidance of the present is usually subconscious, as is the fear that drives it. The apostle John said, *"Perfect love drives out fear"* (1 John 4:18). Fear is a powerful and painful emotion that can single-handedly derail our spiritual quests. *"Perfect love"* is oneness with God. When Jesus said, *"Be perfect, therefore, as your heavenly Father is perfect"* (Matt. 5:48), He was referring to a reality that is in the scope of human participation only to the extent that this oneness with God is realized. A miraculous proof of John's statement concerning love casting out fear is that the dissipation of fear is a certain result of persevering in the practice of these principles.

One component found in this and all the steps is trusting God. In the Bible, *believing* and *trusting* are usually synonymous. For the secularly minded person, however, this is not the case. Like the word *love, belief* could refer to a number of things. It is not unusual for a person to "hear" a commonly known verse like John 3:16 say, "Anyone who really *thinks* that Jesus is the Christ will eventually be rewarded with eternal fellowship with the heavenly Father." Biblically speaking, however, to believe is to *trust*, which is the cornerstone of any healthy relationship. When taken to the divine-human level, trust becomes a recognition of our absolute dependence upon God. There is a well-worn anecdote, silly though it may be, that illustrates the biblical concept of trust. It goes as follows:

> Suppose you witness an acrobat performing the amazing feat of crossing a canyon on a tightrope while pushing a specially-designed wheelbarrow filled with three fifty-pound bags of dry concrete mortar mix. The tightrope walker is famous for having performed this feat dozens of times. If someone who had not seen the feat asked you if you believed the acrobat could do it, you would no doubt answer "yes" with a considerable degree of certainty. However, if you were asked to trade places with the bags of mortar in the wheelbarrow while the tightrope walker performed his feat, that is where *trust* and "belief with certainty" part ways.

Persistently seeking God's will and doing it is what this step is all about, and it requires persistent trust. The most difficult part of this step, however, is trusting God for the results of our actions. We constantly struggle to make things happen. In so doing, we are likely to miss the mark of God's will because our focus is on the outcome rather than the means of our actions.

Remember when you were a kid how difficult it was to understand the principle, "It's not whether you win or lose, it's how you play the game"? Well, that may be how you feel about the notion of working toward a goal as though the results of your work are your sole responsibility while, at the same time, completely trusting God, rather than yourself, for the results of your actions. Like most of these principles, you can waste time and energy trying to figure it out, or you can "just do it" and enjoy the understanding that will result. There are some very important reasons, however, for trusting God, rather than yourself, for the results of your behavior.

First and foremost, as is the purpose of the first step, your relationship with God is dependent upon your recognition of the fact that you are operating in absolute dependence upon God.

Second, when you force results, you operate on your own power with behavior that is self-centered. Self-centeredness is based on fantasy. One of the most persistent enemies of spirituality is the delusion that we have more power and control than we actually have. Quite simply, micromanaging outcomes is the antithesis of trusting God.

Third, your expectations predict how you will manage the results of your behavior. For a detailed discussion of that problem, refer to chapter 6.

Finally, controlling anyone or anything beyond the scope of you, and your own behavior, just doesn't work. You can be lovable, for example, but you cannot *make* the object of your affections love you. You can provide a nurturing, consistent, and disciplined environment for your children; but, while in all likelihood they will grow up to be fine adults, there are no guarantees. When it comes to the results of the many actions you take, there is often an infinite number of variables affecting the final outcome.

You can't make the object of your affections love you.

Based upon your most humble understanding of God's will, you have both the ability and the responsibility to do everything within your power to encourage a good and positive outcome. However, you are not only *not* responsible for the outcome itself in a given situation, but because you are not God, you have no way of knowing precisely what the ultimate outcome *should* be. How often have things actually turned out better because you didn't get your way? And what a relief and freedom it is that we do not have to be, nor should we be, the governors of our own small universe. The willingness to do our part in the many relationships in life to the best of our abilities, while completely trusting God for the results of our efforts, is perhaps the most difficult part of this step, including the exercising of raw perseverance. Yet it is, in fact, the most liberating aspect of our third principle, and the relief it provides carries over into every aspect of our spiritual quests.

A Seventh Case Study

It was not unusual for Chaplain Freeman to return from lunch to find fifteen or twenty basic trainees seated on the pew-like benches fastened to the walls of the large chapel reception area. Some of the trainees still wore their "civvies," which meant they were still in their first several days of basic training. Some had the look of relief at the privilege of a few breaths away from the nose-to-nose, in-your-face stress of their training instructor (TI). Some faces wore expressions of utter defeat. With few exceptions, their withdrawn looks demanded, "Get me out of here!"

The motivation behind volunteering for military service varies from money for college to getting out of the hopelessness of an inner-city neighborhood to just plain leaving a comfortable, middle-class nest to make the final transition to adulthood. Few of these trainees will actually drop out. They merely need a word of encouragement and perhaps a reality check that their military careers will be nothing like an extended prison sentence of harassment in Basic Military Training School.

Phillip was a tall, handsome nineteen-year-old with slightly Asian features, a baby-smooth face, and a soft, almost feminine voice. He gracefully slid into the chair facing the desk, waiting, as if for permission to break the silence. Numb from the assembly-line flow of basic trainees, the chaplain said with the warmth of an answering machine, "Hello, I'm Chaplain Freeman. May I help you?"

"Well," and then Phillip paused, "I didn't realize there would be so many waiting to see you. I guess because I was the only one in my squadron to ask for a permission slip."

"Don't worry; we've got time," replied the chaplain half-heartedly.

"I really don't have a problem. I do need some help, though. Several of us guys in the squadron get together for prayer just before lights out. We asked the TI if we could have a few minutes of Bible study during that time, and he said it was okay just as long as it didn't interfere with our duties or schedule. He said that we could have fifteen minutes."

"That's interesting," said Freeman cautiously. "I've never heard of anyone doing that in basic before, but if that's all right with your TI, I think it's great."

Phillip and Chaplain Freeman talked for approximately forty-five minutes, which was a long time for personal attention from anyone in basic training. The chaplain provided Phillip with a devotional guide for his Bible study and several Gideon Bibles. Phillip was one of only two people in his squadron who packed a Bible for basic.

As far as the superficial characteristics of pop culture that would mark Mr. Popularity, Phillip had none. Basic training is designed to build team players, but it is also extremely competitive. It is designed to prepare groups of people for war, and we all know what war is. Before his training was through, he would face one or two Rambo wanna-bes with his Gomer Pyle aura. With thousands of basic trainees in his care, Chaplain Freeman worried about Phillip enough to occasionally visit Phillip's squadron. Careful not to draw attention to this fine, idealistic young man, the chaplain revealed nothing of his concern to Phillip's superiors. He simply hoped that his occasional presence would remind Phillip of his support if the young man needed him.

The Sunday before the squadron's graduation came much more swiftly for Chaplain Freeman than it did for Phillip, but there the young man was in the very first pew, flaunting the graduating privilege of wearing his blue uniform for the first time. He wore the same uniform and smile as his classmates, with one exception. To the chaplain's surprise and joy, Phillip wore the coveted award ribbon identifying him as Honor Graduate. The chaplain had had only a brief encounter with Phillip. Perhaps that's one reason why the chaplain seemed to be the only one surprised. Chaplain Freeman's later conversations with Phillip's TIs revealed that the confidently humble, soft-spoken young man was virtually unsinkable. Unlike Daniel of lions' den fame, Phillip's peers respected him for courageously and consistently choosing the high road. Like Daniel, he earned the admiration of his direct, nose-to-nose superior. (See Daniel 6.)

Our discussion of this third step opened with the proposition that most people have experience with some form of perseverance. Indeed, Phillip's classmates persevered in order to complete basic training. But another point that has also been emphasized is that, with the exception of Step One, before ascending a step, one must be firmly grounded in the step(s) preceding it. Without being familiar with *The Promises* as listed here, Phillip was definitely familiar with practicing the principles themselves. His persevering meekness was definitely of the third-step kind. His TI, by the way, sat in on and enjoyed Phillip's Bible studies on several occasions. Step Three, like all *The Promises,* cannot be ignored. And what's so special about godly perseverance? Endurance is merely a matter of hanging in there. Its satisfaction is found in the light at the end tunnel. "Persevering in the present," on the other hand, produces a steady, confident stream of satisfaction because the present is where the Great I Am reveals Himself, and that one-day-at-a-time experience is what unconditional joy is made of. (See Exodus 3:14.)

Chapter 9
Making Amends

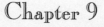

Blessed are those who hunger
and thirst for righteousness,
for they will be filled.
—Matthew 5:6

4. We have joy doing whatever is necessary to *make amends*, in righting any wrong we have done to others, provided it is in their best interest, with no regard to any wrong they may have done to us, trusting that God will reward us with a deep sense of satisfaction.

This, the most demonstrable of these steps, may be the most likely to be dreaded. It is nevertheless the one that provides the most immediate satisfaction. There are few experiences in life as rewarding as confidently facing someone you have wronged with a genuine and thorough proposal of *amends*. Such a prospect is possible only if you are in the process of the previous steps. There is also the importance of understanding the meaning of an amend. Before we thoroughly address what constitutes an amend, however, let us say that it is basically "righting any wrong we have done to others...with no regard to any wrong they may have done to us."

Hungering and thirsting for righteousness may seem on the surface to mean always wanting to be right, but such an interpretation is both incorrect and has often been used by perfectionists (in the dysfunctional sense) to achieve more harm than good. In perhaps Paul's most theologically charged letter, the one to the Christians in Rome, he addressed as his theme the righteousness of God (1:16–17). By contrasting it with God's wrath against the way we human beings pervert the natural order of things (1:18–32), he demonstrated how, if we are willing to *"live by faith,"* God will literally transform our miserable ego-centric failures into redemptive victories. (See Romans 2 and following.) To *"hunger and thirst for righteousness"* means that we do our part in righting the wrongs we have done. God takes care of the rest.

First of all, "doing whatever is necessary" to accomplish this noble aspiration both contributes to the joy of doing it and is absolutely necessary for the prevention of being sidetracked from your purpose. Anything less than total commitment to this step will likely ensure the derailing of the process at some point. Your attempt to make amends carries with it no guarantee that it will be welcomed, or even received. Nevertheless, your attempt to right the wrongs you have done is as important to your spiritual well-being as is the correction of the inequity itself. If making amends to the extent advocated here is more than you bargained for, let us return once again to a review of the alternatives.

Doing whatever is necessary to accomplish what is perceived as a necessary goal will not be new to you. All of us have awarded "necessity" status to a myriad of things that are actually luxuries. Working in much the same way as a classic addiction, often our slavish devotion to the maintenance of these luxuries becomes the very shortcut that sabotages our spirituality. For example, people may spend the majority of the waking hours of their adult lives in jobs they do not like in order to fund the economically dangerous shopping sprees that serve as diversions from the professional lives with which they are so dissatisfied.

Some people leave their spouses and even sacrifice their children for the romantic attention they crave. Addicts who would normally play by the rules, were it not for their addictions, steal and even commit violent crimes in order to get a fix. An example that is much less extreme and is all too common is the workaholic striving for an unquenchable brand of self-esteem at the expense of the very family he or she claims to be working for. There are even those who focus on temperance in all matters to the point of repressing the uniqueness of the human personality. The point is that human beings attach themselves to perceived, though unreal, necessities. It is natural for us to pursue something toward which we will go to any lengths to have and to keep.

Unfortunately, this is not true of spirituality. We must consciously choose and perpetually recommit ourselves to a relationship with God. This is because, while our attachments may thrive alongside and even feed off of one another, God will not compete with them. He requires that His devotion be reciprocated. Considering the *"price"* with which we have been *"bought"* (1 Cor. 6:20; 7:23), doing whatever is necessary to right any wrongs we may have done to anyone is a small requirement for the maintenance of our spiritual health. The fact is, we have a wealth of experience—some of which we are unaware—in going to costly lengths to realize certain accomplishments. Now we have the opportunity to apply our determination to an accomplishment that will reward us with that indescribable sense of satisfaction and well-being that we refer to as unconditional joy.

An Eighth Case Study

Noland had been exceptionally thorough at making amends. In most cases, he directly faced the person he had harmed with a confession and a sincere apology. To those with an active role in his life, he made an effort to correct anything less than his best behavior. He rightly made the decision not to contact an old flame whom he had caused considerable emotional pain. To do so would have been inappropriate since they were now both married with families of their own.

Noland's former Monday-night-football, beer-drinking buddy was now his closest confidant and partner in *The Promises*. It is a rare worldly friendship that transcends into a spiritual one. Both men had ascended to the fourth level together and rather quickly. Competition can be a good thing, but it has no place in the practice of these principles, and it wasn't a problem here. The problem was that Noland was stuck at Step Four. His friend was squarely in the business of doing Step Five, and it was apparent to both that Noland, despite rewarding gains and a satisfying taste of unconditional joy, was backsliding. The old ego-centric, pre-Promise Noland was rearing his ugly head, creeping into familiar strongholds. He began to feel that he could do with a lot less of all the things that had comprised his spiritual progress, including Bible study, church participation, and frequent phone calls with his confidant. He was even slacking off on the attitude of gratitude.

It was half-time on a Monday night, and Noland's friend was in the bathroom washing his hands. As he reached for the hand towel, the designer impression of Holiday Inn reminded him of Noland's unusual collection. At one time, Noland had boasted that he had collected at least one full set of towels from every hotel, motel, and roadhouse in which he had ever stayed. Nowhere was it mentioned in his moral inventory, and he certainly had not addressed the situation in his fourth step amends.

When confronted, Noland responded with the predictable rationalizations, like "ripping off" motel towels is an American tradition, everyone does it, and hotels expect that and have it built into their prices.

One cannot be exposed to *The Promises* for an extended length of time without eventually being able to see through lame excuses. But Noland held his stolen collection dear. It motivated him to count this little chink in his armor as unworthy of attention. Subconsciously, though, he knew better, and bathrooms adorned with stolen terry cloth would eventually take their toll.

It was a hassle, not to mention expensive, to return all those towels and washcloths to their rightful owners. Recipients included corporate offices, individually-owned operations, and linen services. Some recipients were inspired by Noland's honesty and sense of conscience. Others thought he was an inconvenience or a nut. But for his sake, it had to be done, and he did it—even sending generous checks for those items too worn to be returned.

If you are experienced at this point in the first three steps, you probably understand the power of the combination of the humility, effort, and slate-cleaning to propel Noland forward on the right track. An insignificant object can jam and halt a mighty generator. Honesty about ourselves requires that we leave no stone unturned. Or to put it still another way, some amends may seem much more significant than others, but a thorough housecleaning is always the rule of thumb. Just ask Noland, who is as enthusiastic about his unconditional joy as he ever was about Monday night football.

In making amends, the willingness to do whatever is necessary to see it through is paramount for it to truly be accomplished. What most people consider amends is no amends at all. Rather, it is either simply an apology with excuses, or even self-righteous overtones, or it is an attempt to right a wrong from the perspective of the offender rather than that of the offended. Furthermore, few people even consider making amends unless they themselves are directly affected by their wrong. When the victim resists, bristles, or retaliates, an amends by either party no longer seems appropriate. It is amazing that people get along as well as they do.

As your experience has no doubt taught you, making amends often seems inappropriate, pointless, or even risky and threatening. Therefore, it is understandable that "righting any wrong...to others, provided it is in their best

146

interest, with no regard to any wrong they may have done to [you]" would seem at first glance to be a fanatical, extreme imposition. However, if you have persevered in taking Step Two by courageously evaluating your moral condition, you know that that activity is much more than "digging up the past."

You will discover that settling all moral accounts to the best of your ability is necessary if you are to proceed in growing spiritually and in experiencing an ever-deepening, ongoing joy. To put it simply, you cannot follow through with your part of your relationship with God unless you are attending to your part of your relationship with other human beings.

Lest you become discouraged with what may seem to be a daunting task, consider these encouraging words.

Making amends is both rewarding and energizing. Jesus said, *"Come to me, all you who are weary and burdened, and I will give you rest....For my yoke is easy and my burden is light"* (Matt. 11:28, 30). Upholding your part of your relationship with God is both rewarding and energizing. What is both futile and exhausting is when we step over the line into God's part of the relationship.

One of the first lessons of the first step is the liberating and refreshing fact that we are responsible *only* for ourselves. We are, of course, responsible *to* others in our lives, but God is responsible *for* everything and everyone else. Likewise, in the fourth step, we are freed and even protected from any of the garbage or chaos on our neighbor's side of the street. Our amends, whether accepted by our neighbor or not, is the act of our own housecleaning. Being responsible for only our side of the street is empowering because, unlike when we tried to control people, places, and things, now we have the much simpler and more realistic task of sweeping only our side of the street. We are focusing, for a change, on something we can do something about.

Imagine how healthy and secure your job, school, church, or family would be if each individual within those groups stopped taking each others' inventory and concentrated exclusively on their own spaces. While this, of course, will never happen, being true to these principles, you can bask in healthy and rewarding behavior on the comfortable landscape of your own property, regardless of the condition of that of your neighbor. If you are willing to channel to your own housecleaning a mere portion of the energy you have spent on attempting to control the uncontrollable affairs of others, you will soon find that what seemed to be a daunting task, namely that of making amends "with no regard to any wrong [that] may have been done to [you]," will become one of life's most rewarding pleasures.

You are responsible for your side of the street.

Now, how do you make amends? Again, Jesus said, *"You have heard that it was said, 'Love your neighbor and hate your enemy.' But I tell you: Love your enemies and pray for those who persecute you"* (Matt. 5:43–44). Some late manuscripts include Jesus saying, *"Bless those who curse you, do good to those who hate you"* (v. 44 NKJV). Whether or not the latter is authentic to an eyewitness account, it is certainly in keeping with Jesus' teaching.

An enemy is one who is a real or perceived threat to us. When you wrong someone, you make that person a real or perceived threat to you whether he or she was originally or not. An amends should be preceded by prayer, and rather than for yourself, it should be for the person with whom you will attempt to set things right. The Promise states, "provided it is in their best interest." While your amends is a self-imposed function of your personal spirituality, you are never to strive toward spiritual progress at someone else's expense. Your prayer for and amends to the injured party are always to reflect their best interest, as you understand it.

For example, if you have a boss who is an overbearing micromanager, rather than to pray that God will change this individual's personality and/or leadership style, you may pray that this person may be promoted or that specific stresses in his or her professional and/or personal life will be lifted. Likewise, when you approach such a person face-to-face, who very well may have provoked you to take some regrettable action, you identify and apologize for your wrong without eluding in any way to any wrong he or she may have done at any time and/or for any reason to you. You make no excuses, you do not grovel, and your follow-through is not determined or affected by whether or not he or she accepts your apology. In addition to your apology, your amends includes your intentional changed behavior toward that person. Consider the following illustrations.

Examples of Making Amends

You are convinced that you are underpaid and that your employer has no intention of offering advancement to you. Therefore, you pad the expense account and take office supplies home for personal use. It is not enough to confess your transgressions, saying you are sorry and that it will not happen again. You come forward with the money or supplies in hand—or a down payment on a plan of commitment whereby you will repay your employer in full.

A second example: your preoccupation with work causes your presence with and support of your daughter, particularly in important events in her life, such as her first dance recital or a planned vacation, to be tentative at best. To say you are sorry for missing an engagement and that you will try not to let it happen again is hardly enough. You will provide her with a direct apology to be sure, but you will back your apology with an immediate follow-up. You must reorganize your priorities to the point that you not only increase the quality of time with her, but also provide her with a greater quantity of your time. This may require as much as a reduction in pay or a change in jobs. Not only will your daughter benefit from your sacrificial adjustment, but you will also relish the spiritual pleasure of discovering the treasure of your child. Difficult though it may be, this simple adjustment of priorities will contribute to a new set of values that will help to nurture all your relationships. Remember, spirituality is about relationships, and only relationships have genuine intrinsic, eternal value.

A thorough working of Step Two, in which you "courageously evaluate [your] moral condition," will provide you with a generous list of candidates with whom you will want to make amends. You may no longer have contact with some of these people, and others may have passed away. This may be where you first realize that the primary beneficiary of your amends will be you. It makes no difference whether or not your amends are received. There might be a case in which your attempt to make amends is rejected outright, and you may be dealt with rudely, crudely, and with contempt. Your recipient's response is not your responsibility, nor is it to directly affect your spirituality. What is important to your spirituality is that you keep your house in order with no regard to the condition or response of your recipient.

The primary beneficiary of your amends will be you.

In a third example, consider an amends to an unrepentant person against whom you retaliated, but who died before you either had the capacity or the opportunity to make things right. The following situation is a scenario of parent and child. It is pathetic, and real life versions of it are all too common.

Imagine that you were often neglected by your dearly departed mother. A rageaholic, she abused you occasionally when you were small. As an adolescent, it did not seem to matter whether you were in typical immature form or sincerely trying to please her; her rules and standards seemed arbitrary, and her criticism was nothing short of verbal abuse with which she would cut you to the quick. You loved her, hated her, and needed her approval desperately. The act of your leaving the nest was tormenting and emotionally violent for you and her. Throughout your adult relationship with her, she blamed you for the lack of a relationship. Now her remains are at a cemetery that you have not visited since the day of the funeral. Given this dismal scenario, Are amends necessary? Are they even possible? The answer to both questions is a resounding "yes!"

Making amends is likely to be done with relative ease, and you will have some grasp of the value and wisdom of doing it, provided that you have honestly worked through the previous steps. In making your amends, you will want to be intentional enough to actually visit a site where images of your mother's presence will be enhanced. For many people this would be at the grave. However, if you have access to it, you may want to make your amends in a house you and your mother once shared. In other words, if possible, choose a place where damage to your relationship with your mother was done. The point is to make the experience of the amends as vivid as possible.

In a circumstance like this, it may not be as difficult or as painful as you might anticipate, because you are approaching the task in humility, with the knowledge of your own inventory, and you will be armed with the realization that you are doing the right thing. Your amends will not only be the genesis of repairing at least your part of this broken relationship, but you will no doubt recognize a freedom from the weight of destructive baggage that has haunted and influenced other relationships with which you have had difficulty.

"Doing whatever is necessary to make amends" is an exercise of freedom from resentments. A resentment is that previously mentioned cancer to your spirituality. For many Christians, resentments are, at best, in remission. In performing Step Four, you will be allowing God to remove them altogether. With regard to this mother-child scenario, "with no regard to any wrong they may have done to [you]" means that you make no excuses for your own negative behavior and that you don't assign any blame to your mother. Blame, like resentment, is of no value to you or your mother, or anyone for that matter.

Your personal amends may not resemble these three illustrations. However, in making any amends, there are three basic rules of thumb. First of all, from the day of the amends forward, you will change your behavior toward the recipient in such a way that you demonstrate having his or her best interest at heart. Suppose you have a brother, for example, who by virtue of his personality naturally rubs you the wrong way. He pushes your buttons, sometimes without meaning to, but he does deserve your occasional attention, and you know you should provide it if for no other reason than that he is your brother. In this situation you will neither seek to develop unrealistic close ties, nor will you avoid him altogether. If you have repeatedly avoided him, you will no longer do so. Your tolerance of and even interest in him will become a healthy spiritual exercise in humility. At the same time, you will not devote your companionship to him in such a way that the resulting tension could disrupt your spirituality or damage your relationship with him. On the other hand, if your relationship with him is strained such that he prefers to have nothing to do with you, respecting his feelings and wishes will include honoring that desire.

In addition to being willing to change your behavior for the better, a second rule of thumb is to avoid *any* reference to your recipient's shortcomings, including alluding even remotely to any contribution he or she may have made to the straining of the relationship. For example, returning to the illustration of your relationship with your imaginary brother, in your apology for avoiding him, you would in no way

Avoid any reference to your recipient's shortcomings.

allude to the fact that he pushes your buttons. He probably knows it and may bring it up himself in the course of the conversation. You will want to allow him to carry his apology to whatever extent he deems necessary, but you will avoid at all costs agreeing with him to the point that you dilute the focus of your primary concern, which is to make your part right in the relationship. Remember, you are making your amends based on the findings of your personal moral inventory, because it is the right thing to do. Just as your spiritual progress can be derailed by your taking someone else's inventory, even the hint of it during the making of an amends may actually reverse the result your amends was meant to accomplish.

A third rule of thumb is perhaps an extension of the first, but it should be dealt with separately. The first rule is that you be willing to go beyond a simple apology to actually changing your behavior toward the recipient of your amends, with his or her best interest at heart. The third rule is that you never make your amends, or attempt to nurture any aspect of your spirituality for that matter, at someone else's expense. For example, you would not apologize for jilting a former lover if that person is in a new relationship that may be even remotely threatened by your brief reappearance into his or her life. Likewise, you would not, in the name of honesty, confess the gory details of deviant behavior to your parents, or of unfaithfulness to your wife or husband. This you have already done in the taking of Step Two when you confessed your sins to a carefully chosen confidant who had the ability to reciprocate in the sharing of experience, while being somewhat emotionally detached. It is as tempting and easy to punish someone with the truth as it is to hurt him or her with deception and lies.

As you can see, Step Four, making amends, works hand in hand with, and is as meticulous as, Step Two, taking your personal moral inventory. Both are perhaps the most dreaded of the steps; yet many agree that of all the steps, these two provide the deepest sense of well-being and satisfaction.

Chapter 10
Demonstrating Compassion

Blessed are the merciful,
for they will be shown mercy.
—Matthew 5:7

5. We have joy demonstrating *compassion* to all, knowing that even at our best, we, too, are in need of it as we trust in God for His mercy.

Spirituality is doing the right thing even when it doesn't seem like the smartest or the most expedient thing to do. It is doing the right thing when you don't feel like it. *Spirituality* is knowing your specific predispositions toward excesses and deficits, and celebrating that, in God's grace, you have choices amid the powerful forces of your human condition. When you have had these experiences, you are ready for *compassion*. When you have not, your understanding of mercy is, in actuality, likely to be arrogant, and your compassion is likely to be enabling. Compassion and self-righteousness are mutually exclusive. That is why you need to bring to this Beatitude the solid foundation of Steps One through Four, on which you are firmly grounded in empathy, humility, and gratitude.

In some ways, Step Five will be the easiest and most natural of the steps because your transforming behavior will have inspired the heartfelt motto, "There but for the grace of God go I." You are encouraged to allow your gratitude to compel you to help those who are less fortunate: weak or strong, beautiful or grotesque, rich or poor, mentally challenged or brilliant—anyone in need of what you have. Humility will empower you to discern between right and wrong while being free of self-condemning judgment. Empathy will provide timing and the place for your service as His witness. Allow this chapter to bring true compassion into focus as it applies to your behavior.

A Ninth Case Study

Marci was a respectable, seasoned confidant to several women in her Promise group and with good reason. She exuded an incredible joy and serenity amid some pretty rotten circumstances.

Like so many, her track record prior to her spiritual awakening had been feelings-based and driven. A rescuer by nature, she landed a real loser who abused her and their son until he was gracious enough to leave them.

As a hard-working, resourceful, single mom, with a little help from her aging parents, Marci raised her boy to become the man she always wanted, but never had. She thought he hung the moon, until he fell in with the wrong crowd. She was traumatized at how he seemed to turn into his father overnight. He never physically or verbally abused her. He loved and respected his mom, but not enough to save himself. Marci became enslaved to bailing him out of debt and brushes with the law. It wasn't until her nineteen-year-old faced a possible prison sentence that she discovered the power in admitting powerlessness.

Extremely motivated for her own sanity, with commitment, determination, and armed with trust, meekness, and humility, Marci "let go and let God." No more draining her financial resources to defend the indefensible, her delinquent son. He did the crime. With her blessings, he would do the time.

He was shocked at his mother's tough love, but he never doubted its genuineness. Marci was faithful in her trips to visit him, unlike his fickle friends, and hers were never "guilt trips." She had forgiven him. She had forgiven his father. While he was coming to grips with "the wages of sin" in prison, she was discovering, through a faithful practice of *The Promises*, what resentment-free, guilt-free joy was all about.

Her son served only a year and a half of a three-year sentence. In some ways, the experience left its scars on him. In more ways, it left him better. He stepped from prison into freedom knowing that no human being loved him like his mother. She taught him that even she could not love him like his heavenly Father. She was taking care of her side of the street. It would be up to him to take care of his—and he did.

From the standpoints of cultural, political, and religious history, it may be argued that people are more compassionate today than in any other period of Western civilization. It is difficult for us to imagine imposing some of the merciless consequences of the past upon ourselves or applying them to others. People caught in an abusive marriage were trapped. A child born out of wedlock was forever marked. Alcoholics were considered hopelessly weak, and criminals simply evil. Life was simpler then, but one might also argue that it was cruel. Was life, however, crueler than it is today? A generation ago "the good old days" were lamented. Today we are taught disdain for "the good old days."

"Throwing the baby out with the bath" is perhaps the most apt description of where this disdain has led us morally. A chaotic order unfolds in which everyone from politicians to TV sitcoms are celebrated for their irreverence. Basic education has evolved beyond the three "R's" in order to take on the broader categories of developing self-esteem and preparing our children for life. This, of course, is done with an intentional effort to substitute a faddish, politically correct agenda for time-tested moral values.

Individual rights take center stage only if they represent some sort of deviancy, and tolerance becomes its own brand of bigotry. What is often paraded as compassion is little more than "cutting the deviate some slack" or enslaving the less fortunate in dependency upon inadequate handouts. In contrast to a secular notion of compassion, God's mercy is bestowed both unconditionally and with tough love.

Anyone can give lip service to "caring" or "feeling your pain." A key to a genuinely compassionate level of Christian living is that you *demonstrate* compassion. As with each of the steps, you must *do* something. In the case of this fifth step, you are to do whatever is in your power to bestow love, particularly upon those who least merit it. We have already been reminded of Jesus' shocking words: *"Love your enemies, do good to those who hate you, bless those who curse you, pray for those who mistreat you"* (Luke 6:27–28). As was stated in a previous chapter, enemies are those who pose real or perceived threats to us. Jesus is not suggesting that we "feel" affection for such people. For Jesus, love is a choice expressed by action. Feelings are not to be the driving force here. This is quite a different perspective from the secular notion that compassion, and especially love, are emotions.

While the world celebrates love as something one "falls into," Jesus advocates love as an intentional choice of commitment with a purpose. Likewise, while secular scholars may argue that ours is the most compassionate society in history, our Lord requires something quite different from a "touchy-feely" personal emotion that embraces the sin along with the sinner. To the secular heart, compassion is either "live and let live" or simply give people what they want. By the same token, mercy is merely a matter of letting an offender off the hook. For the follower of Christ, compassion involves sharing the tools that provide the means of obtaining what the Bible clearly says that every human being needs—redemption. Mercy never gives up on redemption, but it may require the practice of tough love.

If the unchurched have a favorite Bible verse, it must be Matthew 7:1. Often when biblical standards of right and wrong are referred to as having objective or absolute authority, there is the snide retort, usually from the King James Version: *"Judge not, that ye be not judged."* This is another way of saying, "We all have our faults. I don't plan on any change in my behavior anytime soon. I'll stay out of your business, so you stay out of mine!" In addition to angry criticism here, we are at the threshold of a secular understanding of compassion and mercy.

Role models today, the ones we admire, are not examples toward which we are to aspire. Rather than people we attempt to identify with, they are people we *do* identify with, because they share our flaws, or they "feel our pain." For this reason, we admire Mother Teresa, but we love and cherish Princess Diana. Comfort is found in the notion that stark imperfection is the norm. Though we dare not admit it, even to ourselves, pitiful extremes are nothing less than uplifting. Secular compassion and mercy enable us to "enable" others, as we pity the less fortunate with a faint sense of superiority in which we never have to abandon our self-centeredness.

Who could have fathomed that the generosity of a great society would produce a new class of slaves in which addicts are subsidized with disability payments and fresh needles, people who practice various forms of sexual deviancy are protected as a special class, and the lifestyle of choice for some is homelessness. By the way, a simple litmus test whereby you can determine whether you are in the secularly compassionate, politically correct camp is if the previous sentence has the ring of bigotry and intolerance to you. If it does, then you are in that camp. A further "by the way": let the author go on record as one who firmly supports secular tolerance in that it is the recognition of and acceptance that everyone has the right to exercise personal freedom. Tolerance, however, does not mean that we are to subsidize or support

Acceptance does not mean agreement.

behavior that we in any way find offensive, and acceptance does not mean agreement.

Discussions like these are important because our understanding of these issues helps determine whether our practice of mercy and compassion is a selfish, "feel good" pursuit or the real thing. The practice of the fifth Beatitude is important because it is a fundamental result of the ongoing process beginning with receiving the gift of salvation.

To illustrate both the importance of the fifth Beatitude and how to practice it, let us turn to a passage that is perhaps more familiar to most people than the Beatitudes themselves, and one that is also found in the Sermon on the Mount. Regardless of your familiarity with Scripture, you can probably recite the Lord's Prayer with no hesitation. (See Matthew 6:9–13.) In that prayer, Jesus refers to our sins metaphorically as *"our debts"* (v. 12 NKJV). Those who transgress against us are *"our debtors."* The Greek word translated *"forgive"* in this verse and the Greek word for *mercy* in Matthew 5:7, while being distinct with independent roots and definitions, both carry the notion of canceling the appropriate debt. When you exercise mercy in the biblical sense, you neither block consequences nor hold a grudge or nurse a resentment. Just as with the previous steps, you are able to internalize the phrase, "There but for the grace of God go I." You neither enable a perpetrator nor condemn him or her. You don't assess the offender's value to God or your relationship with that person. In other words, you forgive unconditionally and absolutely. Furthermore, to whatever extent you may be required to interact with a fellow perpetrator of sin, and we are all sinful perpetrators in one way or another, you act in a manner that demonstrates absolute forgiveness.

Remember, when you are operating at this level of spirituality—that is, the fifth step—you bring to it the experiences of Steps One through Four. You are at once on "active duty" and a seasoned veteran. Regardless of your ability to let go and let God have His way at this point, the important thing is that you have a genuine willingness to demonstrate a truly compassionate quality of mercy. As to exactly how the fifth step is to be acted out, consider the following illustration.

A Tenth Case Study: An Example of Mercy and Compassion

A woman's son is killed by a drunk driver. The driver has the legitimate disease of alcoholism, and he is sincerely remorseful. These facts, of course, offer little consolation to the mother of the deceased. However, because of her experience of the comforting power of the Beatitudes, she is willing to do whatever is necessary to be rid of the hatred and bitterness she understandably feels toward this man. Her desire to forgive does not prevent her from actively participating in the process that results in his being sentenced to twenty-five years in prison. At the same time, she does not position herself to prevent an early release if it comes. She addresses her natural resentment toward the alcoholic with sincere and earnest prayer for him daily. In this particular case, she prays that the alcoholic will find recovery from his disease. He does.

As part of his recovery, he attempts the seemingly impossible task of making amends to the victim's mother. Because of the willingness of both to salvage whatever is possible from the tragedy, the miraculous result of a series of face-to-face meetings is that the recovered alcoholic is released after serving ten years of his twenty-five year sentence, and together the two embark on a speaking campaign to address the consequences of driving under the influence. Thus we have a remarkable example of the age-old tradition of divine inspiration empowering Christian faith to bring meaning and even redemption out of an irreversible tragedy.

Such miracles are commonplace among those who courageously pursue intimacy with God. Demonstrated compassion has the power to heal and liberate. This is true of both victim and perpetrator. At the same time, as in the case of Step Four, where making amends is the order, spiritual restoration is dependent only upon the willingness of the person dispensing mercy, not upon the willingness of the recipient to receive the mercy. The woman who lost her son in the tragic drunk-driver accident, for example, would have recovered to spiritual wholeness, regardless of the decisions and actions of her son's killer, by virtue of her persistent lifting him up in prayer and her willingness to forgive.

It is instructive to note that the "happy ending" of our illustration would have probably not come to fruition had strict consequences not been enforced. This is not to suggest that recovery from addiction or spirituality in general can be forced. Nevertheless, any alcoholic solidly on the track of recovery will testify that "hitting bottom" was a catalyst for his or her return to sanity. That "bottom" may be devastatingly low, such as losing one's job, family, friends, and health, or it may be what is often called a "high bottom," such as the mere threat of a pink slip from an employer. In any case, mercy honors the delicate balance between commensurate consequences and the miracle of absolute forgiveness. By the time you reach the fifth level of your spiritual development, in the form of self-discipline, you will be ready to apply this balance to your own life.

The cross is the ultimate symbol of divine mercy. To be godly is to identify with Christ, and to be Christlike is to extend the same mercy to our transgressors by which we ourselves have been saved. Paul reminded us:

Like the rest, we were by nature objects of wrath. But because of his great love for us, God, who is rich in mercy, made us alive with Christ even when we were dead in our transgressions. (Eph. 2:3–5)

This same merciful God reveals His wrath *"against all the godlessness and wickedness of men who suppress the truth"* by "[giving] *them over to a depraved mind"* (Rom. 1:18, 28). In other words, God does not force Himself on anyone. Neither should we. But He, and only He, enforces consequences with pure justice. Sometimes, to let someone go is the merciful thing to do. It may seem cruel for a parent to refuse to bail a repeat-offender child out of jail or for an entire family to reject an addict member who repeatedly refuses treatment, but to do otherwise is to enable the deviant's destructive behavior.

Whether dealing with others or with ourselves, mercy is shown by establishing clear, godly boundaries, by accepting and following through with appropriate consequences, and by openly displaying the free gift of absolute forgiveness to anyone, including yourself, who by demonstration of repentance is willing to receive it. And what of those who go unrepentant? Well, that's God's business. Long before we approach this delicate fifth step, the spiritual sojourner learns that there is no room in Christ for our resentments.

Chapter 11
Aligning Our Wills with His

Blessed are the pure in heart:
for they will see God.
—Matthew 5:6

6. We have joy allowing our wills to be aligned with His to the point that our *motives* are *pure*, trusting that we will see God's active participation in our actions.

When Abraham Maslow constructed his now-classic *Hierarchy of Needs*, he identified the pinnacle of his construction, "self-actualization," as a level of operation few people obtain. Like any process sustained over a period of time, this is also certainly true of the remaining Beatitudes. The reason is simple: you may have reached this level of spirituality in which you have a firm foothold upon the unconditional joy of a deflated ego, but you will never be able to discard the ego altogether. Neither will you reach perfection in the application of any of these principles. Nevertheless, while "pure hearts" may be rare, even among the most dedicated Christians, do not hesitate to go for this wonderful step. As this chapter unfolds, you will be pleasantly surprised to discover that, if you have come this far, you have been working on this step all along.

An Eleventh Case Study

Walter and Elaine were pillars of the congregation. They had been active members for only about two years, but active they were. They had qualified for senior discounts for over a decade, but they made themselves available to lend a helping hand to anyone or any group of any age in the church. Their effectiveness and popularity stemmed from a simple approach to ministry. They focused their energies on what they could *do* for the building up of the church, not how they *felt* about what the church was or wasn't doing. Helping the body of Christ do His will was their agenda.

In addition, they were just plain cute. In Bible study and worship, they sat scrunched up together like high school sweethearts. They held hands in the parking lot on the way to the car. Young couples would whisper, "I sure hope we're like that when we get old."

When Brother Jim came on board as the new minister to senior adults, one of his first orders of business was to get a handle on a celebration the congregation had been planning for Walter and Elaine's fortieth wedding anniversary. He thought he misunderstood when Walter remarked, "Yeah, Elaine and I have had thirty-six wonderful years together."

"I thought we were celebrating your fortieth wedding anniversary," questioned Brother Jim.

"You're right," said Walter. "Next Tuesday we will have been married forty years, and thirty-six of them have been great!"

Now Brother Jim wore an "explain what you mean" expression, so Walter continued.

"About ten years ago, Elaine and I started drifting apart. It got to the point that the only time we spoke was to criticize and argue. Elaine would nag, and yet she wondered why I didn't want to have anything to do with her."

Smiling, Walter continued, "I asked her what she wanted for her birthday. She said, 'A divorce!' I told her I hadn't planned on spending that much. Actually, neither one of us thought we could afford a divorce. We had invested the best years of our lives in the marriage and not giving our best shot to salvage what was left wouldn't be fair to the children, grandkids, the marriage, or to us.

"We attended this church when the children were growing up, so we came here to the pastor for help. Are you familiar with *The Promises*?" Brother Jim responded with something about Promise Keepers to which Walter said, "No, not that," and went on.

"*The Promises* are kind of like a step program, except they're based on the Beatitudes. Anyway, Elaine and I have been doing the steps ever since. We were in misery for two long years, and once we started this program, it took us almost two years to get out of it. But, through it all, we found the Lord, and we're closer than we've ever been in our marriage. Thirty-six good years out of forty. Pretty good, don't you think?"

Spouses with healthy, intimate relationships and people who share intense, committed friendships sometimes report thinking like their partners to the extent that they know, with reasonable certainty, how the other would respond in almost any given situation. In conversations, they are virtually able to complete their partners' sentences. Such is the relationship with God for the pure in heart. Most Christians will have a glimpse of this throughout their growth process. This quality of relationship is extended to all who are in Christ. **What is** The recipients of the gift of salvation, as the **God's will** objects of God's love, have before them the **for me?** strenuous, but pleasurable, task of ever emptying themselves of self so that the flow of God's infilling goes unimpeded. Despite the fact that most of us rarely operate at this level, it represents the fundamental question all followers of Christ have from day one: what is God's will for me?

Consider the viewpoint from which you have asked this question. Were you seeking direction for a choice of vocation? Were you hoping for some sort of assurance in the planning of an activity? Did you expect an identifiable confirmation of a commitment you had made? A Christian college student appeared to be a career undergraduate because he was "waiting for the Lord to lead [him] to the right major." A lonely, middle-aged single adult hopelessly held out for God to place Mr. Right in her path. While such concerns may indicate spiritual sensitivity, their pursuit as these individuals' primary focus actually detracts from or stunts the spiritual growth of their relationship with God and with others by diverting them from the very foundation of experiencing the Lord's intimate leadership in their lives in the present. God does not fuel a college student's procrastination or sentence a single adult to loneliness. Nor does He shroud their life choices in mystery.

By the time you have reached this, the sixth step, you know from experience that when you persevere in tending to the important personal relationships—divine and human—then vocations, commitments, and daily activities fall amazingly into place. Remember, *"in all things God works for the good of those who love him, who have been called according to his purpose...to be conformed to the likeness of his Son"* (Rom. 8:28–29). It is easy to forget that God is as concerned with our wills as we should be with His. That is why practicing the Beatitudes is itself "allowing our wills to be aligned with His to the point that our *motives* are *pure.*"

We are co-participants with Christ.

When we apply these biblical principles to all we undertake, we discover that we are no longer subjects waiting for divine orders. We are co-participants with Christ as members of His body (Eph. 4:11–13). This being the case, let us concisely review and identify what constitutes each of the previous steps as set forth in *The Promises.*

A Summary

Remember, it is God's will for you to experience unconditional joy. You do this by praying consistently a prayer of thanksgiving in any and all circumstances (1 Thess. 5:16–18). This means that you acquire a schedule for prayer, meditation, and the development of your personal gratitude list, examples of which are set forth rather thoroughly in chapter 3. Whether you bring the *attitude of gratitude* to the initial practice of the Beatitudes, or you experience gratitude as a result of practicing the seven steps, gratitude will always result in joy and vice versa.

As you have worked the previous steps thus far, you have not only received specific directives, but you have hopefully taken liberties to be personally creative in applying these principles to your individual needs and personality. There is no one way to correctly practice these principles. For that reason, many of the suggestions have primarily focused upon common pitfalls in attempts to undertake this new way of life. The principles themselves are requirements of the Christian life, but these guidelines of how to put them into practice are only suggestions. From the vantage point of experience, the following suggestions may not seem so outlandish and may actually make sense. The bottom line is that they are only suggestions, but they are suggestions that work.

Step One

From the outset, honesty, accountability, and openness are primary ingredients of your response to God's invitation of an intimate relationship. After all, *"God demonstrates his own love for us in this: while we were still sinners, Christ died for us"* (Rom. 5:8). If you have reached that watershed experience providing you with the motivation to admit that you are powerless over sin and that only God can rescue and protect you from your self-centered condition, make a beeline to the nearest Christ-centered, Bible-believing fellowship, and submit yourself to their procedure for making your salvation experience known, whether it be coming forward or speaking with the pastor after the service. Again, submit, submit, submit. This will become a chief characteristic of your new way of behaving. You are not in any way acting blindly. You are choosing

Submit,
submit,
submit.

to submit. Heretofore, many of the things you thought you controlled, in reality, controlled you. Now you have a choice. Your submission to God and to the body of Christ, as opposed to a lesser god, things, or self, is your choice. What a humble, yet powerful, place to be!

Your fellowship of believers will require that you be baptized. There is only one baptism (Eph. 4:5). If your discovery of this program marks a spiritual awakening of your faith, as opposed to a conversion experience, and you have already been duly baptized, you will not want to repeat it. Seek instructions as to baptism's meaning, purpose, and relevance to you. There is not enough room for a discussion of that here, but there are sound reasons why baptism is not optional for the follower of Christ.

As the first Promise states, you are to humble yourself "in all matters." You are not being asked to eat "humble pie." You are requiring yourself to do certain things you would not normally do in your self-centered condition. In many cases these things will actually go against the grain of your nature. However, do not only refrain from avoiding them; seek them out. For example, perhaps it is just not your nature to clean up thoroughly after yourself. Despite complaints, you would be perfectly satisfied leaving a used coffee cup in the sink for days. If such is the case, it's time to have a "spiritual" experience. When you finish your coffee, rinse the cup, place it in the dishwasher, and move on to clean the sink and the countertop—you are doing something not because you have to or because you want to, but simply because it is the right thing to do. The act of submission to healthy behavior, and the willingness to do that which is other than your own will, is an act of spirituality.

By the same token, you may be a compulsive cleaner who will rejoin the conversation of company only after the dishes are done. As uncomfortable or even painful as it may be, this is your opportunity to consciously choose to leave the dishes in the sink until the fellowship is over. By choosing to provide uninterrupted attention to others, over and above a task that can be tended to later, even if it means that dried-on food will be more difficult to remove, you are putting first things first, relationships above tasks or things, which is in and of itself a spiritual experience.

It's time to have a spiritual experience.

In addition to submitting to baptism and other requirements of a body of believers and intentionally seeking out opportunities to go against the grain of your normal self-centered behavior, consistent involvement in personal meditation and devotion is an absolute must. If you are following the suggestions in the chapter entitled "The Attitude of Gratitude," you are already well on your way. Nevertheless, these suggestions are designed to occupy only approximately 30 minutes of your day. Few people do or think about one thing at a time. It is so natural that you probably don't notice as you drive to work that you are listening to the radio while at the same time making plans for later in the day. While working around the house you are thinking up a shopping list, worrying about a troubled friend, and listening to the news from the television in the next room, all simultaneously. It is certainly within the realm of your ability to memorize and recite Bible verses you find comforting and personally relevant as you go about the business of the day. Somewhat gradually, but in a very short time, you will be able to do this while you pray as a source of exercising an awareness of God's presence in your life. Eventually, it will be second nature to pursue these aspects of your spirituality while, at the same time, responsibly going about your day's work.

Finally, by all means, relive your initial salvation experience. Living in the past is not healthy, but remembering what is important is. You might also remind yourself that if you have undertaken the first step, you are living your salvation experience at this very moment. This is all a part

169

of what it means to live in the present while embracing the past and facing the future fearlessly.

Step Two

Are you ready to step up? Only you know for sure. However, don't wait to take this or any other next step until you feel like it. Again, spirituality is not about acting on your feelings. Rather, it's about relationships and your choice to do the right thing within those relationships, and feeling good about your choice and action as a result. Furthermore, people are often derailed in their spiritual pursuits because they are too cautious or slow in moving forward in their spiritual progress. Rarely does anyone ever fall by the wayside, however, because he or she charges full steam ahead.

Chapter 7 details suggestions for putting your introspection on paper. Don't hesitate or try to do it perfectly. Just do it. Remember, your inventory is for your eyes only **God has a** (except for God's) and what you choose to **miracle with** share with your confidant. This brings us to the two most difficult aspects of the second step. For most people, nothing short **your name** of a miracle will: (1) empower them to be **on it.** courageously honest with themselves, or (2) enable them to bare their findings with another human being. God has such a miracle with your name on it, provided you are willing to plunge right in.

There is no single correct way to take Step Two, but unless you know of a proven way other than that which is contained in chapter 7, follow its step-by-step instructions as faithfully and thoroughly as possible. Accept no imitations and avoid, at all cost, any easier way. Like anything, the more you put into the second step, the more you'll get out of it. Be nitpicky. Your little hand in the cookie jar may prove to be more revealing to you about your personality and character defects than some sort of teenage sexcapade you've always been ashamed of. Leave no stone unturned, record your findings in black and white, and know that God is pleased with your willingness to see yourself as you really are. What may seem at times to be a pointless exercise in unearthing the past is in reality the embryo of developing pure motives. Thus, by the time you reach the sixth step, you will have already thoroughly been working on it.

As for your confidant, suggestions have already been made of possible candidates. Even with the most courageous and diligent research of the past, it will be virtually impossible for you to be fully awakened without the aid of another person bearing a substantial dose of objectivity. Choose someone you trust and respect, but not necessarily someone you like. By all means, do not choose a bird of a feather or someone who will tell you what you want to hear. In addition to helping to clear your vision, your tough love confessor will help you to exercise much-needed humility.

Step Three

Step Three is about perseverance. You probably don't need to be reminded that there is much more to this step than just hanging in there. The extent to which this step is practiced determines success or failure. Living the Beatitudes is a progressive, cyclic, and simultaneous experience. Regardless of whether you are researching the past or aligning your will with God's in anticipation of a future result, your experience must be grounded in an acute awareness of the present, because life happens only in the present tense. That being said, you may be interested in trying the following paradoxical exercise.

In the early stages of your spiritual quest, as in the first year, allow your demonstration of your commitment to your relationship with God to include an abstinence from commitment or major decision making to anything outside that relationship that is not absolutely necessary. Changing jobs, buying a house, or pursuing a new relationship will spell needless stress and distraction from your spiritual focus. Unnecessary commitments also provide an outright diversion from your course. In fact, in your communion with God, through prayer and meditation, avoid making promises. They border on bargaining with God. Simply make yourself available to God now. Living one day at a time or, in some cases, one moment at a time, you will be amazed at your ability to abstain from temptation while sustaining behavior that is reinforcing, and even self-perpetuating, your new life in Christ.

Step Four

There are few deliberate acts that you can perform that are more godlike than "doing whatever is necessary to make amends." Not that God has anything for which to make amends. The fact that He has gone to such extraordinary lengths in the person of Jesus Christ to reconcile us, His rebellious creation, for no apparent reason other than an unfathomable quality of pure love, reminds us that our most formidable gesture of Christlikeness is glaringly pale by comparison. Yet, if we understand the righteousness of God in terms of His activity of righting our wrongs and bringing victory out of defeat, what could be more certainly in the will of God than our "doing whatever is necessary" to correct "any wrong we have done to others...with no regard to any wrong they may have done to us"?

If you are following the suggestions in chapter 9 on how to take this fourth step, you are on the right track. In making your amends, remember, at the very least, three things: (1) When you admit you're wrong in the form of a verbal apology, make every effort to avoid even alluding to any wrong your recipient may have done. (2) Count the recipient's response to your gesture as irrelevant to the spiritual necessity of what you are trying to do. At the same time, demonstrate sensitivity by refraining from an attempt to make amends at someone else's expense.

And (3) if further contact with the recipient is necessary, be sure to back your verbal amends with corresponding behavior appropriate to the relationship.

Step Five

There is nothing extraordinary about occasionally experiencing the sentiment, "There but for the grace of God go I." A few, however, ascend to a spiritual plain whereby genuine humility is consistent enough that such a motto becomes a frame of reference or overall perspective. The tenth chapter, containing Step Five, may well be referred to as the "tough love chapter." You are a genuine practitioner of tough love provided you apply the principle first and foremost to yourself. Usurping its personal applications borders on "mean-spiritedness" and/or hypocrisy. Demonstrating compassion leads to your awareness of and the need for the removal of the "beam" in your own eye when confronted with the "speck" in that of your neighbor's. The ensuing attention to personal housecleaning helps prevent you from becoming a busybody, poking your nose where it doesn't belong, or attempting to control what is truly not your concern. You are nevertheless available to help others and are qualified to do so because of your self-examination, the resulting humility, and your personal example of victory. Jesus' compassion stirred His passion for His mission on the cross. Acute empathy for the universal desperation of the human condition cannot coexist with apathy. If you are living the fifth Beatitude, you are sharing the gift of salvation. If you are a fifth-step wanna-be, there is no better place to start than intentionally sharing your faith.

Step Six

If you have been practicing this review, you have been doing the sixth step, pure and simple. It is an intentional internalization of the divine frame of reference undergirding the practice of these principles. You do not simply seek pure motives; you *have* pure motives. This is not to suggest that in this life you are once and for all "sanctified" in perfection. Abandoning any one of the previous steps constitutes a slip into a lower plain. Letting your practice of the steps slide altogether will land you where you were, or worse than where you were, before you started your spiritual quest. This is not a challenge to the various notions of the security of the believer. It is a reminder, however, that *"faith without deeds is dead"* (James 2:26).

Denial is usually the first or major obstacle preventing the first step. Selective memory is the reoccurrence of denial over the course of a lifetime. By the time you have come to Step Six, the lure of sin and the denial guarding it are not nearly as intense as they once were. Yet sin is ever present, often waiting patiently in the recesses of our character, cunningly ready to rear its ugly head. Operating at the level of alignment with God's will takes the time required of the steps and their resulting maturity, but once it becomes your modus operandi, it will feel so right. You will have the confidence, courage, and sense of security, even in the most anxiety-producing situations.

Of course, overconfidence can make us vulnerable to veering slightly off course into what may ultimately prove to be an entirely different direction from our Lord's original intent and purpose. It is therefore helpful to periodically reduce your now somewhat elaborate prayer life to the simple, *"not as I will, but as you will"* (Matt. 26:39). Or, *"Thy will be done"* (Matt. 6:10 KJV). Or, as Step Eleven of the Twelve Steps of Recovery puts it, pray "only for knowledge of His will...and the power to carry that out." You'll be amazed at how spiritually therapeutic it can be, especially when you have a list of requests and concerns, to discipline yourself to the simple prayer, "Please Lord, give me knowledge of Your will for me and the ability to carry it out." As is so characteristic of the miracle of spirituality, occasional strict adherence to this prayer alone will reaffirm the freedom and riches of your place in God's plan.

One final note concerning "allowing [your will] to be aligned with His." Challenge daily your understanding of God's will with what is revealed through His Word. At the outset of this invitation to intimacy with God, you were encouraged to align yourself with a Christ-centered, Bible-believing fellowship. Go beyond the prescriptions of your fellowship's Bible studies and Sunday school classes. With the abundance of excellent devotional guides available, you are bound to find one with scriptural direction that speaks directly to you. Also, occasionally try reading a short New Testament book like James or the gospel of Mark in one sitting. Ultimately, if you adequately apply the first five principles to your life patiently and consistently, you will actually be taking this joyous and rewarding sixth step of faith.

Chapter 12
Peace and Serenity

Blessed are the peacemakers,
for they will be called sons of God.
—Matthew 5:9

7. We have joy pursuing *peace* and accepting *serenity* as the result of these steps, trusting that the Prince of Peace will declare us heirs of the kingdom.

We are but fragile frames for our souls. Because the emptiness is within, it may frequently go undetected. But it is there, it is vast, and it contains chambers filled with junk, litter, and abandoned dreams. Remember that this void was created to be filled by God and God alone. It has taken us time, persistence, and the ascension of six spiritual steps in order to know beyond a doubt that it is the ego that is the culprit. Once, and even along the way, we heavily guarded what we thought was self. Now we know that it is ego, and that it is counterfeit and poor company indeed. At this stage we no longer think less of ourselves. We simply think of ourselves less. We have resigned playing God, removing ourselves from the center of our universe, letting go of the obsession and compulsion to control the uncontrollable; and as we step aside, "Oh, what a relief it is!" Step Seven completes the circle of healthy humility. There is an unexplainable sense of joy and serenity from the very moment we genuinely demonstrate "letting go and letting God."

A Twelfth Case Study (My Story)

I became a baptized, born-again believer at age nine. I surrendered my life to the gospel ministry at nineteen. Because my ordination took place on my twenty-first birthday, you might say that I've been a minister of the Gospel all my adult life. But it was not until age thirty-nine, thirty years after my initial commitment to follow Jesus, that the revealed wisdom contained on these pages took shape for me. The result of internalizing these truths by applying them in my day-to-day behavior has been the unconditional joy I am compelled to share with you.

From the moment I decided to follow Jesus, I wanted to do His will, but I just never seemed to "get it." In retrospect, God's faithful and persistent leadership in my life is without question. It has been said, "It takes what it takes." For me, it took all my experiences, including self-inflicted pain, to reach the threshold of my current spiritual pilgrimage.

Like you perhaps, I had experienced inspiration and desperation, happiness and heartache. The instability of it all was more than I could bear. I had thrown myself into all sorts of diversions in order to get out of myself, including the noble one of my profession. But at age thirty-nine, at the height of my military career as a chaplain in the United States Air Force, preaching to over four thousand basic trainees on any given Sunday, being pressured for my "counseling skills," and hanging awards on my "I love me" wall, my self-centeredness landed me on the brink of a nervous breakdown.

Unlike me, my wife Michaela has a kind of natural spirituality about her. She became acquainted with the Twelve Steps of Recovery when she and several of her nine brothers and sisters sought help coping with alcoholism in their family. It was obvious to her that recovery principles provide solutions to all sorts of problems and that I had become one big problem in need of a solution. Everyone knows you can't teach your spouse how to drive, and

Michaela had no illusions that she could teach me to be spiritual. Instead, she introduced me to Buddy Bradshaw, a person she was sure I would respect and like. A decorated Air Force retiree with over twenty years of personal Twelve Step experience, he conducted a family counseling ministry in which he used recovery principles to treat all kinds of spiritual, emotional, and behavioral maladies. Through his patient friendship and the help of his colleague, John Posch, and of course the faith and long-suffering of Michaela, the truth of *The Promises* began to take shape as I discovered the wonderful connection between the Twelve Steps and some things I had learned in seminary.

As a student, two courses were of particular significance in this regard. One was devoted exclusively to the Sermon on the Mount with an in-depth emphasis on the Beatitudes. The other was a course in pastoral counseling that included study of the application of the Twelve Steps. The counseling professor explained how the Steps provided a spiritual antidote to the alcoholic's and addict's craving for self-induced euphoria, a handy tool for someone like me who would be counseling someone like them. Regarding the Sermon on the Mount, there was an excellent devotional book by the same title in which Dr. Clarence Jordan described the Beatitudes as the "stair steps to the kingdom." In that class, it seemed as though I wrote a ream of notes on each Beatitude regarding historical and theological information and life applications. If, at that time, I had distilled each ream into a single sentence to summarize the Beatitude in question, I would probably have come up with steps very close in meaning and purpose to those of *The Promises*. But I had to reach a point of hurting desperately in order to make the connection. I had to go beyond a cognitive simulation to a willingness to simply follow directions.

These *Promises* are perfect for a hardhead like me. It was not as though Michaela offered help, the light came on, and voilà, I became a new creation. No, time and setbacks preceded often humble victories. By the time my narcissism had come to a head, our marriage was held together by raw commitment to God's law. Had divorce been an option, we would have taken it. And what if we had? Would our thirteen-year-old son be the well-adjusted young man he is today? Would he have the security of being with both Mom and Dad, together, each evening? Would he be the unintimidated witness for Jesus that he is with his peers? Would he have had the self-confidence and stick-to-itiveness to earn a black belt in karate? (Oh yes, I like to brag.) And what about Michaela and I? Back then, when our marriage was on the rocks (instead of being on The Rock), we didn't know that today we would be one another's head cheerleader, that we would relax in one another's warm embrace, or that we would share a limit-less ministry of unconditional joy. We didn't know these things back then, and at times we didn't even have faith. But we did have hope. More important, we had willing-ness, and most of all, God took what we offered Him and filled it to the brim and overflowing.

The Hebrew word for *peace* is used so frequently inside and outside the Old Testament that its transliteration, *shalom*, is a familiar English synonym. In both the Hebrew and its Greek counterpart, it may refer to something as simple as the absence of conflict; however, its basic and broadest meaning, when applied to a spiritual state of being, is *wholeness*. The natural craving for this wholeness is so powerful that every human malady can be traced to some sort of misdirection of its pursuit. Substances are used as an attempt to provide relief on demand. Hollow pursuits for meaning, excessive pleasure, and recreation spun out of control are those counterfeit and all-too-brief diversions discussed so frequently on these pages. Dysfunctional relationships provide anything but whole-ness, and they fill the vast empty spaces only because they need so much room in which to malfunction.

Peace means wholeness.

When we consider the exhausting energy required to fortify our delusions and function in a consistent state of retreat from reality, the seemingly stringent demands of the Beatitudes are but a cakewalk. Much was made in the previous chapter of the rarity of ascending to the sixth step. As was also stated, it is beyond human ability to consistently practice any of the steps with perfection. Those who ascend ultimately to this level develop enough genuine humility along the way to know and accept this. Everyone experiences setbacks. Nevertheless, in spite of setbacks and bruising falls, those who practice Step Seven are the ones who trudge gratefully and joyfully forward. While few people experience genuine wholeness, it is a gift extended to all, and one desired, received, nurtured, and appreciated by those who take *The Promises* full circle.

Peacemakers are the only ones in the Beatitudes given a title. Although too much may be made of this distinction, titles, as with names, were very important in the first century. More than a label, titles and names were intended to embody a person's characteristics. With the power of self-fulfilled prophecy in their upbringing, people often took on the qualities of a given name, as was the case from Israel's beginning. (See Genesis 25:26.)

"Prince of Peace" is, of course, a title of the Son of God. Jesus said that peacemakers will be called children of God, but He was not suggesting that we become God's children as a result of obtaining a particular level of relationship with Him. Our adoption into God's family, with both its privileges and responsibilities, is God's gift to us from the moment of our commitment to Him (Gal. 4:4–7). What the seventh Beatitude does tell us is that peacemakers will be *"**called** [the] sons of God"* (emphasis added). In other words, peacemaking will be an identifiable function of both their work and their nature. You can never remind yourself too often that the Beatitudes embody actions we are to take as followers of Christ. At this level, a fundamental question of the seventh Beatitude is, therefore, How do you make peace?

The answer: *Share with others the gift of wholeness that you have received.* You can give only what you have.

Likewise, salvation is not something to be contained. The late cofounder of Alcoholics Anonymous, Bill Wilson, described his discovery of spirituality as a vein from which we can mine limitlessly provided we give our treasure away. You may have heard the joke about the minister who skipped Sunday morning worship to play golf and got a hole in one. His punishment was that he wasn't able to tell anyone. Similarly, even the most timid of believers have a natural desire to share something as dynamically wonderful as the gift of salvation. **Share the gift of wholeness with others.** This basic form of evangelism begins in the infancy of the spiritual experience and is most contagious. However, by the time you have developed into Step Seven, there is more than the message to share. You have wholeness and the miracle of your personal transformation to back it up. From the moment you took that first step, you were new all over again (2 Cor. 5:17). Not only did God bless you in your willingness with a stick-to-itiveness to forge a new pattern of behavior, but you also began to catch a glimpse of the joy of operating from a whole new point of reference.

"Pursuing peace and accepting serenity" are two facets of what it means to be a peacemaker. Peace doesn't just happen. It's something we actively pursue. In other words, it involves conscious action, as do the previous steps. In the wording of this Promise, there is no significance in the shift from the word *peace* to that of *serenity*. There is a distinction, however, in the emphasis of *accepting* serenity in addition to *pursuing* it, in that as the result of all our spiritual actions, serenity is a gift from God to us. These two sides of peacemaking also serve as a reminder that, as with all aspects of spirituality, we can share only what we have.

Our Role Model

Our role model is not an angel or a character from a parable or an illustration. Our role model is a real Person in history. Jesus of Nazareth is the historical ideal by which human wholeness is to be understood. As the embodiment of 100 percent God and 100 percent human, Jesus Christ resides both in the intimacy of His relationship with His followers and beyond any subjection to intellectual examination. Nevertheless, the historical Jesus displays a variety of behavioral characteristics that together serve as a wholeness to be emulated. The following examples contain singular biblical references and are not intended to be either exhaustive or broad.

Any thorough commentary will address the question, If Jesus is God, how could He be genuinely tempted? Most commentators will deal with this issue in conjunction with an examination of Jesus' temptation in the wilderness. (See Matthew 4:1–11.) If you care to research them, depending upon the commentator, you will be given the choice of a variety of approaches to this question. They will not be researched here. However, it is my opinion, contrary to some otherwise good commentators, that there are no limitations to God. While it is often argued that God cannot sin or that His nature forbids Him from acting in any way contrary to love, my belief is that it is important and helpful to understand and experience God as limitless. He does not love us or "chase" us because He *has to* as the result of His nature. God determines His own nature. God is the One who defines sin. In the context of our discussion of the topic in previous chapters, sin is anything contrary to God's will. Second, God can choose, do, or be anything. One must reach for a theological construct outside the biblical realm in order to conclude that Jesus' temptation, as One who was truly human, was anything less or of a different kind than that which we face. The miracle of God's presence in the person of Jesus of Nazareth is that, for whatever reason, He chose to love us to the extent that He deemed it necessary to somehow squeeze Himself into our shoes and walk infinitely farther and more faithfully in that capacity than we are able to fathom.

You cannot save the world; Jesus can. Your temptations are finite, while His are mounted on a grand and infinite scale (although anyone's submission to seduction carries with it the potential of infinite consequences). Jesus' three wilderness temptations (Matt. 4:1–11), as they relate to us, were to live for gratification of natural human desires (vv. 2–3), to put God to the test (vv. 5–6), and to barter His spiritual birthright for the glory of the present, while serving the creature rather than the Creator (vv. 8–9). Jesus' responses, both in the desert and as these temptations manifested themselves throughout His ministry, were simple enough to be emulated by any spiritual pilgrim. Let us briefly examine Jesus' responses of quoting Scripture, imposing self-denial, focusing upon His mission, and pursuing quiet time. There are also the issues of His control and use of the emotion of anger and the coping skill of humor, as well as His demonstration of other common behavioral characteristics.

You cannot save the world; Jesus can.

First, Jesus met challenges by quoting Scripture, which meant He was grounded in it. You cannot maintain serenity while nurturing character defects or meandering into dead ends of diversion. Think of how many behavioral wrong turns could be avoided if each excursion of the day was met by even a casual consultation with the road map of God's Word. Serene habits like Bible study and prayer are born not so much out of discipline as they are from sheer desire. You do not need to be a monk or a mental giant to read the Bible or pray. Regardless of how well you do them, or how comfortable or natural they feel, these are simply things you do because doing them is right.

Second, Jesus met challenges by imposing self-denial. The revelation that Jesus was *"led by the Spirit into the desert"* (Matt. 4:1 NKJV) attests to His willingness to submissively provide us with a thorough example of self-denial. Jesus never commanded fasting, but He practiced it. He also gave guidance for doing it (Matt. 6:16–18). Any expression of self-limitation as a means of intensifying your conscious contact with God is an extremely effective form of prayer. It may be argued that Jesus' fasting set the stage for His temptation in the wilderness, a deliberate act of preparation for the more persistent and subtle temptations that were to dog Him for the rest of His life on earth—which leads to a third point.

Spirituality involves a calling to a mission. As has already been emphasized, your mission is to pass along to others what you have received. As One called to and focused upon His mission, Jesus did not set sail unprepared, and neither should we. A frequent diet of self-imposed delayed gratification builds trust, discipline, and confidence. Just as a tree needs soil, rain, and sunlight in order to grow, serenity flourishes only when our actions foster trust, discipline, and confidence. These are not prerequisites, but rather results of your willingness and desire to respond affirmatively to the outpouring of God's presence in your life.

Fourth, Jesus went away to be alone with God (Luke 4:1; 5:16). Likewise, our calling as followers of Christ requires that we operate within the world while not being *of* the world (John 17:14–19). Quiet time becomes increasingly valuable in the noisy world of the information age. God's rewarding use of our lives as redemptive agents in an anxious, overpowering, high-tech landscape will no doubt include the use of the technical creations of our hands. Sunday school teachers will use online computers to help them craft their lessons. Satellites will carry the Gospel to the ends of the earth.

Nevertheless, in a culture where people can hardly jog or mow their grass without the aid of noise-polluting headphones, regularly leaving the cell phone in the glove compartment and shutting down TVs and computers are minimum requirements for "pursuing peace and accepting serenity." Remember, our narcissistic receivers have enough difficulty hearing the voice of God over the polluted static of our hearts. The frequent removal of obvious diversions from our spiritual quests is the least we can do.

In addition to these character traits exemplified in Jesus' behavior, there are other examples that demonstrate His wholeness. In the Sermon on the Mount, Jesus addressed the emotion of anger. Similar to the way that sexual desire is capable of developing into lust, so anger has the capacity to escalate into murder of the heart. (See Matthew 5:21–30.) Yet it is significant to recognize that, while Jesus warned against the dangers of anger, He neither denied its reality nor was reluctant to direct it toward threats that were potential obstructions to the will of God. Jesus provided a particularly graphic example of an appropriate use of anger in His scathing "Woes" to the Pharisees and the teachers of the law, as well as in the familiar account of His cleansing of the temple. (See Matthew 21:12–13; 23:13–39.)

"And being in anguish, he prayed more earnestly, and his sweat was like drops of blood falling to the ground" (John 11:35 NKJV). He was physically shaken to the point that He actually requested the preference of His human will, to be spared the agony of the Cross. Yet, in keeping with His third and sixth Beatitudes, He persisted in conscious contact with the Father, and He persisted in doing God's will (Matt. 26:39). Can emotional pain exceed that associated with abandonment or rejection? When the weight of the rejection of humanity came crushing down on Him in the ultimate isolation of the Cross, our Lord did not hesitate to, once again, quote Scripture in an open display, free of pride, of His anguish and loneliness (Matt. 27:46; Ps. 22:1).

Peace, then, may refer to an absence of violence in some scriptural references. But it did not necessarily mean that for Jesus, and it does not necessarily mean that for the Christian who has ascended to the level of peacemaker (Matt. 24:9).

A sharp line of distinction has been drawn between the experiences of happiness and joy. Given the somberness of our study of Jesus thus far, you may wonder, "Where is either?" In actuality, Jesus exemplified one of the most effective coping skills and peace-rendering characteristics of all. The quality, usually absent in portraits and other characterizations of the Master, is a sense of humor. Whether gleaned from biblical accounts or from an artist's caricature on canvas, apart from a few fairly recent exceptions, the earthly Jesus most Christians know is one who laboriously trudged through every waking hour of His ministry, facing rejection at every turn, and who operated ceaselessly under the depressing weight of the sins of the entire world, with only a cross upon which to rest.

If these qualities were all that were available to us, we would not have as our role model a healthy human being, much less a portrait of the Prince of Peace. As any student of psychology will tell you, humor is an excellent barometer of one's mental health. If all we knew about Jesus was limited to His teaching in the Sermon on the Mount, we would still have at least three obvious examples of the comedic side to Jesus' earthly personality. Read the brief passage of the Sermon (Matt. 5–7), and if these humorous illustrations do not jump off the page at you, it may very well be because of your own personal, subconscious, religious preconditioning to filter out any comic relief associated with either the Lord Himself or the Bible in general.

The three examples of Jesus employing the technique of humor to drive His point home are these **Jesus used** in the order of their appearance: (1) light**humor.** ing a lamp merely to place it under a bowl; (2) drawing attention to and trying to help remove a speck of sawdust from a neighbor's eye, while being impaired by a plank in your own eye; and (3) giving sacred and treasured items of great value to unclean, unpredictable, and unappreciative, ridiculous recipients. Consider first, if you will, a sample of Jesus' humorous technique and, second, the essential place of humor in spiritual growth.

When employing humor to make a point, timing is everything. Of the three above examples, the one most obviously illustrative of this technique opens with a famous and favorite command of many opponents to organized religion, who themselves judge its many expressions as a sea of hypocrisy. As has already been stated, they quote the King James Version: *"Judge not, that ye be not judged"* (Matt. 7:1). What these critics, treating bigotry with bigotry, are actually saying is, "Mind your own business!" They use Jesus' own words to purport the very opposite of the point Jesus was making. There are certainly types of judging that are off-limits to the Christian. Refer, for example, to John 7:24; Romans 14:1–5; 1 Corinthians 4:1–5; and James 2:1–4.

But in Matthew 7:1–5, Jesus is warning specifically against the hypocrisy of our condemnation of someone whose problem or fault is similar and equal to or less than our own. Note how He carries the emotions with perfect timing from the serious to the hilarious, then in one fell swoop (by calling the judgmental "hypocrites"), to the deadly serious again. What an extremely effective way to emboss in the listeners' memory that they are in fact to help the person with obstructed vision; but *first*, through honest self-examination, they are to make sure that their own sight is clear. You can, of course, see the relevance of Step Two.

Have you seen an old black-and-white comedy or early TV sitcom lately? Perhaps it was a rerun from the original production that first ran decades ago. You may have noticed that it did not seem nearly as hilarious the second time around. That is because of the way our thought processes have been reprogrammed with the evolution of technology. As was discussed earlier, our attention spans grow ever shorter as we become accustomed to receiving practically all our information in visual flashes and sound bites. Depending upon the joke, the timing of the punch line may be different today than it was several decades ago.

In Jesus' day there were no comic strips, sitcoms, or comedy clubs. Jesus' perfect oratorical skills could hold a multitude spellbound for hours on end. His word pictures provided graphic animation for their minds' eyes. The cartoonish picture of a character with a pole stuck in his eye while trying to help someone whose vision was impaired by a mere speck no doubt sent an eruption of roaring laughter through the audience. Whether you think it is hilarious or not, you can be sure Jesus' listeners did. But of course there is no mention of laughter in the text because the seriousness of the point is what is important. Jesus' comic prowess speaks for itself.

Pardon the pun, but a sense of humor is serious business because it is nothing less than necessary for emotional health and inner peace. Think of anything humorous—a joke, a personal experience, something that happened to someone else, anything. Note that if it was funny in any way, at some level it dealt with the tragic, the embarrassing, the stupid, the painful—some negative life experience. In some cases, the more negative or out of character, the more humorous the scenario. A homeless or physically-impaired person stumbling is not funny. Rather, it provides a pathetic picture. A pompous politician stumbling on his way to the podium is a hoot. Topics of humor range from issues like innocent blunders to something as serious as death. But whatever the scenario, humor has the power to suspend the most threatening consequential act in time, thus removing its sting by momentarily elevating us to a spiritual vantage point.

This is not to suggest that humor in and of itself is spiritual. Nothing is in and of itself spiritual. Sex, for example, is not, and yet, while it is often the object of perversion as with a dirty joke, it has the capacity to be one of the most divinely ordained spiritual experiences of intimacy imaginable. Likewise, humor in its proper place is as necessary to our spiritual and emotional equilibriums as a healthy inner ear is to physical balance. Jesus, of course, was not only without sin; He was without blunder. Therefore, He had no reason to laugh at Himself. We, however, would do well to develop the ability to step back and amuse ourselves by seeing our ridiculous ways and circumstances for what they are. The ability to laugh at oneself is truly a gift from God, an outgrowth of humility, and an ingredient of inner peace.

Humor, by its very nature, is meant to be shared, and so it is with God's gift of peace. Once you have received peace, it is yours for as long as and to the extent that you give it away. If, for a moment, humor shields us from the withering anxiety of the relentless marching of time, serenity lifts us to the level plane of eternity, where security is the norm and joy is unconditional. Peace and serenity are both qualities and results of being embraced by the everlasting arms of God.

Chapter 13

Joy

Blessed are those who are persecuted
because of righteousness,
for theirs is the kingdom of heaven.
—Matthew 5:10

Our Lord promises that the practice of these principles will insure our joy in the midst of even the worst possible circumstances, for ours is eternal, abundant life.

There is one more step. Like the first step, it does not build upon a previous one. Unlike the previous steps, it may be appropriate to address at any point of your spiritual pilgrimage. In the first step you stopped fighting or attempting to manipulate sin; in the second step you pursued a thoroughly honest personal moral inventory; and so on. Unlike the others, the eighth Beatitude does not describe an action step that you initiate. Rather, it promises a condition of joy in the core of those who are persecuted because of an outward expression of their faith. In the first century, this would have applied to nearly everyone within the sound of Jesus' voice who would heed His call to discipleship. There are many places today where religious persecution is still very much alive. In the luxury of freedom and religious tolerance, it is difficult to shake the denial that at this very moment, there are people being tortured to death for their faith in Jesus Christ. In a free society, Christians deal with this step in more figurative terms.

Americans in particular have, for the most part, a Lone Ranger mentality. They are joiners, to be sure, of churches, clubs, fraternities, teams, and parties. But most feel relatively comfortable moving from one organized group to another, depending upon the evolution of their personal or family values or views and/or their particular needs regarding socialization.

For the masses throughout history, however, as has already been mentioned, such has not been the case. People, for the most part, have seen themselves as rather insignificant parts of the greater whole. This was certainly the mind-set, during the first century, of the vast majority of the many worldwide cultures under Roman rule. Within the barely distinguishable separation between the politics and religion of Judaism, there were Sadducees, Pharisees, Essenes, and Zealots. Many a rabbi had his own following, and a few were themselves self-proclaimed messiahs. While there was always strict tension between the religious establishments and groups—like Christians and followers of John the Baptist—many of these groups could survive for a while as bona fide Jewish sects.

Nevertheless, all these people guarded as sacred both their relationships and their identities with their families, communities, synagogues, culture, and nation in geographical, practical, and historical terms. It was one thing to stand proudly as a Jew against the condemnation of formidable international pagan forces, and quite another to risk rejection by one's own people. Unlike many today whose ultimate human pursuit is the avoidance of physical and emotional discomfort, people back then faced such issues as suffering and death with relative confidence and a sense of purpose. What was difficult to assimilate spiritually and emotionally was risking the rejection of the very people from whom they drew their identity. All the more torturous was the notion of being rejected for "righteousness' sake."

Such an experience would affect emotional stability in much the way a child would be scarred by being repeatedly punished for behaving well. That is why Jesus' encouragement included a reminder that those who would suffer because of Him would be in the good company of the prophets before them. Indeed, their immersion into the Christian life as set forth in the Beatitudes was grounds to *"rejoice and be glad"* (Matt 5:12), "even in the worst possible circumstances." After all, as the apostle Paul would say, *"If God is for us, who can be against us?"* (Rom. 8:31).

Jesus' physical death on the cross was so painfully horrendous that to concentrate on its specific details would be sickening to even the most callous person. However, rejection by the very fickle human beings to whom Jesus came to save was perhaps the most painful part of the equation. The One in whose name we pray knows firsthand the worst possible circumstances—rejection, physical pain, temptation, grief, anxiety—and all the emotions that are appropriate responses to them. He was without a doubt addressing the momentous obstacles, such as vicious, violent rejection, that the first Christians would face as they presented themselves as *"living sacrifices"* (Rom. 12:1) in the birth and formation of the church as the body of Christ. Yet how much more does this promise of joy apply to us as our faith is tested in the arena of our own comparatively minor "worst possible circumstances"? Again, as Paul would say, *"Neither death nor life...nor anything else in all creation, will be able to separate us from the love of God that is in Christ Jesus our Lord"* (Rom. 8:38–39).

We live in a world where the worst possible circumstances will happen. We do not need to go looking for them. We *should* not go looking for them. Looking to persecution as a litmus test for being in God's will, will seduce us off course with poor judgment and the allure of pride as surely as if we were motivated primarily by ease, or by warm, fuzzy, pleasurable sensations. Jesus did not go looking for a fight; neither should we. To do so is to bring discredit upon ourselves, others, and the cause of Christ.

The danger of a martyr complex is one reason why the eighth Beatitude is not set forth here as a step, per se. A second reason is that, unlike the previous steps in which we do something, the eighth Beatitude describes our confidently joyful response to that which is done to us. A third reason is that daunting obstacles may appear at any time. This is not a level at which we make preparation for tragedy to strike. It describes what we will be like when it strikes. We have the resources to triumphantly face both the bad and the good, because from the moment we trust God to rescue and protect us from ourselves and the forces of evil, we share in Christ's victory over sin by His life, death, and resurrection; and our relationship with Him includes our partnership with all believers.

As a side note, don't underestimate spiritual vulnerability to the "good" temptations, such as success, fortune, or advantage. Some people are at greatest risk when life is at its best. Lest we make the mistake of the recovering alcoholic who is so pleased with his sobriety that he loses it in a moment of celebration, we should be as grounded, humble, and intentional in our embrace of blessings as we are with obstacles and tragedies. In other words, the solution to this tricky dilemma is staying close to God by the simple process of working the seven steps.

Chapter 14
The Conclusion?

One More Case Study

Discomfort and pain are facts of life. When we turn to an addictive agent rather than God for relief, we sin. Sin usually does provide temporary relief, but there are always negative consequences at some level. Thus, caught in the vicious cycle of more pain, we once again seek the relief of our substitute for God.

Nerves alert us to physical pain, thereby protecting us from further physical damage. Without physical discomfort and pain, we would constantly be injuring our bodies without knowing it. Guilt provides a similar warning for our spiritual and emotional well-being. The sin cycle churns out guilt as a generator produces electricity. Apart from *The Promises*, guilt is merely a negative consequence that functions as part of the cycle itself. Strangely, when we practice the Lord's principles, guilt becomes a trusted friend. Rather than run from, ignore, avoid, or deny it, we face it, confess it, correct it, and are free. As long as we are earthbound, we will never be guiltless, but by honest self-examination, making amends, and openness to God's forgiveness, we can live guilt-free.

With this understanding of the functional purpose of guilt firmly in place, I was unprepared for Marvin when he approached me for help. Marvin was the first psychopath I encountered since I had become a counselor. Psychopaths are not necessarily serial killers, and Marvin wasn't even particularly mean. He frequently caused trouble, and he'd had several brushes with the law, but, basically, he was your run-of-the-mill, self-centered jerk. At least that's how Marvin described himself. Years earlier, in a self-initiated psychiatric evaluation, Marvin had been diagnosed with an antisocial personality disorder. Neurologically speaking, Marvin simply didn't have the brain function of guilt. According to Marvin, he was unable even to conceptualize the emotion of guilt.

As a "fisher of men," I was always delighted at the prospect of an occasional fish hopping into the boat even before the net had been cast. Well, Marvin had hopped in and was floundering around, and I really didn't know what to do with him, even though he seemed as eager for the Gospel as the Ethiopian eunuch whose path had crossed with Philip's. (See Acts 8:26–39.) I prided myself in demonstrating trust in a God who can do anything. I also believed then, as I do now, that *The Promises* are for anyone willing to embrace them. Or did I? Remember, Marvin's personality profile was that of a criminal type. Also, *The Promises* transform guilt into a prime motivating factor, but remorse was out of Marvin's realm. My job was to share the Gospel and help Marvin take his first step. Instead, I was psychoanalyzing him, and he'd had enough of that.

At first, Marvin's green eyes and thinning gray hair presented a middle-aged man who looked distinguished and somewhat handsome. A second look revealed that he was very tired. At thirty-eight, experimentation with drugs and alcohol had taken its toll on his body, and unremorseful lies and manipulation made him unfit for commitment and intimacy. Tired and lonely, he may not have been able to feel the emotion of guilt, but he was well acquainted with its consequences.

That was it—the key to his motivation. I, in my "wisdom," saw Marvin as my toughest challenge, when in fact he was presenting himself to God, not to me. He possessed both a major advantage and the single most important ingredient for doing God's will. In the first chapters of this book, I pounded away at the importance of breaking through denial and admitting to your living problems. Marvin had been there, done that. Most important, Marvin had then what he has today: the one quality that would assure his participation in *The Promises* and a successful Christian life—willingness. Marvin had had enough of the fast track, grabbing and chugging life with gusto, and living as though there were no tomorrow. Now he was willing to take it easy, one day at a time, in the present, because the present is forever.

Most of us would be overwhelmed with the type, amount, and depth of amends Marvin will be making for the rest of his earthly life. He found it necessary to accumulate three years of spiritual progress before he extended his hand and heart to a potential partner. Today he's not the best husband in the world, but he is a good husband, and his sweetheart wife knows it. They met in church, and they continue to attend church. He is not exactly a dynamic leader, but he has a powerful testimony, and he is not bashful about sharing his Savior with others. Neither of Marvin's parents lived to be proud of their son, but one of the marvelous results of Marvin's amends is that he will one day join them in eternal joy. Only God knows the length and breadth of Marvin's journey before he crosses the eternal finish line (Phil. 3:12).

Typically, *The Promises* transform feelings through focusing on behavior. This approach proved perfect for someone like Marvin, void of the most rudimentary emotions necessary for health. Whether Marvin's was a case of brain chemistry adjusting to his new healthy behavior or a grateful recipient of a new mind in Christ, he is a miraculous example of God doing for him what he could not do for himself, even with the aid of the most advanced techniques in therapy and medicine. According to Marvin, for the first time in his life, he "feels right."

Of the several case studies that have been presented here, on a scale of emotional health, the pre-transformed Marvin would be on one end of the spectrum, while Frank would be on the other. The other cases would be somewhere in between. Regardless of where you fall on the spectrum, God's Promises are for you. Are you willing to accept His invitation?

How does one conclude a study of a life of unfolding meaning, purpose, and joy without end? If you are firmly on course applying the principles herein, you will no doubt return to this material often. New pages will be written with the choices, actions, and discoveries you make.

Illustrative of the unfolding nature of the spiritual process, several years after writing, memorizing, and diligently applying these principles to every aspect of my life to the best of my ability, on one occasion, for no apparent reason, it dawned on me that a form of the word *trust* appeared as a sort of pivotal point in each of the seven steps. This repetition was not intentional, but I believe it to be very significant. In today's vocabulary, *faith* may refer to a system of beliefs, and *belief* may refer to mere speculation. *Trust*, on the other hand, is an action word in which we "let go and let God."

When we apply *The Promises* to our lives, we understand the old cliché, "God helps those who help themselves." We also know from personal experience that "letting go" is difficult, but rewarding, work. By taking to the Beatitudes in such a way that we apply them as intentional behavior, now we can truly say, "We've finally figured it out; now we know how to live!" All the secular education and human intellect we could muster could not open our eyes, even to the simple truth that while we slavishly gave ourselves to the pursuit of happiness, what we really hungered for was unconditional joy. Before, we operated on self-will; now we live according to *God's* will (Matt. 12:50). What used to be complicated, confusing, and frustrating is now a simple matter of "doing the next right thing" to the best of our abilities. By the way, "doing the next right thing" is a phrase borrowed from a member of AA. Here are some other clichés from Twelve-Steppers you might find rich to ponder:

- Live one day at a time.
- Live and let live.
- Anytime I make a big deal of anyone or any thing, other than God, I make a big deal of myself.
- It's hard to keep an open mind with an open mouth.
- Regardless of your worry, remember, this too shall pass.
- Accept life on life's terms.
- Acceptance is not synonymous with approval.
- Make a friend of time.
- Humility is not thinking less of yourself; it is thinking of yourself less.
- The best way to get even is to forget.
- No one is converted by criticism.
- You do not help by trying to impress; you impress by trying to help.
- You can't be hateful when you're grateful.
- Let go and let God.
- Rather than have what you want, seek to want what you have.
- [And, one of my favorites] Lord, help me to become the person my dog thinks I am.

Today I saw on a bulletin board at a YMCA here in Louisville:

Yesterday is history; tomorrow is a mystery.
Today is a gift.
That's why it's called "the present."

Wisdom is everywhere, if we have eyes to see.

These clichés are simple, and perhaps corny, but aren't they great! The bottom line: do whatever is necessary to minimize your ego, utilizing divinely-inspired biblical principles, such as those contained in the Beatitudes, and experience God's infilling presence. Your self-esteem will soar to heights of unconditional joy!

Epilogue
Spirituality at a Glance

1. Unconditional joy is the state of being that *"is God's will for you in Christ Jesus"* (1 Thess. 5:16, 18). It is usually confused with *happiness*, which is an emotional response to external or internal stimuli, such as people, objects, activities, or psychological techniques. Unconditional joy is created by God in you as a result of your relationship with Him and is, therefore, unaffected by circumstances or the environment.

2. The universal search for happiness, meaning, and purpose is based on the reality that human beings are created in the *"image"* of God (Gen. 1:26). This means that you have, at the core of your being, a God-shaped space that only He can adequately fill. Vacancy of this core space is unthinkable. Driven by a threat, conscious or unconscious, of unbearable anxiety, this space must be occupied, either by the ego or God.

YOU — Ego — SELF

in your will
Born in sin, people settle for this—the familiar.

YOU — Holy Spirit — SELF

in God's will
Born for this, it is the state of being that people crave.

3. The healthy self is God-centered. The unhealthy self is ego-centered. The problems revealed through self-examination identify your ego-centric condition. The Beatitudes of Jesus Christ constitute His step-by-step prescription for the healthy deflation of your ego as God takes His rightful place at your core (Matt. 5:3). This progressive process is the essence of Biblical spirituality and is fundamental and necessary for spiritual health.

4. The goal of spirituality is oneness with God. Its process leads to self-actualization (the person God created you to be). The process involves, "not thinking less of yourself, but rather, thinking of yourself less." The cancerous growth of the ego diminishes self-esteem. Life in Christ produces healthy self-esteem commensurate with spiritual growth and progress.

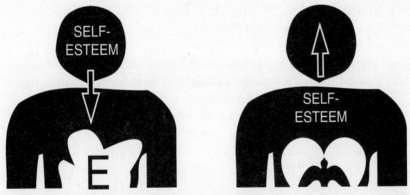

5. There is nothing you can do to merit a saving relationship with God through Jesus Christ, but in order to participate in such a relationship, you must be willing to do what Jesus described in the Beatitudes (Eph. 2:8–10). The Promises simply explain the Beatitudes' requirements.

The Promises

Our Lord and Savior Jesus Christ promises that we will experience divine joy, which is His will for us, to the extent that we take the following steps (Matt. 5:3–10; 1 Thess. 5:16–18; Phil. 4:4; Ps. 68:3–4; 118:24; Gal. 5:22; Neh. 8:10):

1.   We have joy admitting that we are powerless over sin, believing that only God can rescue and protect us, and *humbling* ourselves in all matters, trusting that, because of Him, ours is eternal life (Matt. 5:3; 18:1–4; 1 Cor. 8:2–3; Rom. 12:3–8, 12; James 1:9; 4:10; 1 Chron. 17:16; Mark 9:35; 2 Chron. 7:14; Num. 12:3; Ps. 18:27; 149:4; Prov. 11:2; 22:4; 1 Peter 5:5–6).

2.   We have joy *courageously evaluating our moral condition*, honestly admitting our immorality to God, facing it ourselves, and confessing it to another human being, trusting that we will experience an ongoing sense of well-being (Matt. 5:4; 11:28; Prov. 12:22; Isa. 29:13–14; Mark 7:6–7; Ps. 103:8–13; Heb. 4:16; 1 John 1:5–9; James 4:9–10; 5:16; 1 John 1:9).

3.   We have joy *persevering* in the present, and seeking God's will and His power to accomplish it, trusting Him, rather than ourselves, for the results (Matt. 5:5; 6:25; 11:29; Isa. 4-:28–31; 1 Cor. 9:25–27; 15:57–58; Rom. 5:3–5; James 1:1–3, 12; 1 Tim. 6:11–12; Heb. 12:1; 2 John 1:8–9).

4.   We have joy doing whatever is necessary to *make amends*, in righting any wrong we have done to others, provided it is in their best interest, with

no regard to any wrong they may have done to us, trusting that God will reward us with a deep sense of satisfaction (Matt. 5:6, 43–48; 18:21–35; James 4:9–10; 5:16; 1 John 1:9; Exod. 34:5–7; Neh. 9:17; Col. 3:13; Rom. 12:14–21).

5. We have joy demonstrating *compassion* to all, knowing that even at our best, we, too, are in need of it, as we trust in God for His mercy (Matt. 5:7; 6:14–15; 9:36; Luke 6:36; 1 Cor. 13:4; Col. 3:12; Eph. 2:3–4; 4:2–3; 1 Thess. 5:14–15; James 5:7–8).

6. We have joy allowing our wills to be aligned with His to the point that our *motives* are *pure*, trusting that we will see God's active participation in our actions (Matt. 5:8; Luke 22:42; John 14:26; Rom. 8:5–6; 2 Tim. 2:22; 1 Thess. 5:16–18; Col. 1:9–10; Heb. 13:20–21; Ps. 1:1–3; 51:10; Phil. 4:8–9).

7. We have joy pursuing *peace* and accepting *serenity* as the result of these steps, trusting that the Prince of Peace will declare us heirs of the kingdom (Matt. 5:9; 11:29; John 14:27; 16:33; Rom. 5:1–2; 8:6; 14:19; 15:13; 1 Cor. 7:15; 14:33; James 3:17–18; 2 Thess. 3:16; Eph. 2:14; 4:3; Col. 3:15; Phil. 2:8–9; Gal. 5:22; Jude 1:2; Ps. 4:8; 29:11; 119:165; Prov. 14:30; 16:7; Isa. 26:3; 52:7; 54:10; 57:2).

Our Lord promises that the practice of these principles will insure our joy in the midst of even the worst possible circumstances, for ours is eternal, abundant life (Matt. 5:10–12; Ps. 18:2; 121:1–8; Josh. 1:9; Rom. 8:31–34; Eph. 6:10; Phil. 4:11–13; Heb. 12:2–3).

Guidelines for Building
a Promise Group

Jesus said, *"For where two or three come together in my name, there am I with them"* (Matt. 18:20). So it is when two or more gather to share their experiences, support, and humility in the application of *The Promises*. A Promise group is open to anyone willing to practice them.

The following suggestions will ensure maximum effectiveness in conducting Promise group meetings.

Promise group meetings function best when the following suggestions are observed.

&~ All participants should be practicing *The Promises*, and the members should take turns serving as facilitator of the meeting, rotating each session. Effective exchange requires the shared goals and purpose of those within the group and courageous honesty within the safety of absolute confidentiality.

&~ Meetings should follow an established schedule with a minimum of at least one per week lasting one hour each.

&~ The three basic types of meetings are:

The *discussion meeting* in which seating is arranged in a semi- or full circle, either openly or around tables.

The *study meeting* in which a Beatitude or other Scripture, a chapter from *Unconditional Joy*, or a related text is read aloud and discussed.

The *speaker meeting* in which a practitioner shares his or her personal story followed by equal time for discussion.

ॐ Meetings should have a consistent, functional location, such as a church, home, business, or any regularly available, functional place.

Pitfalls to be avoided are as followed:

ॐ Participation in a Promise group is not a substitute for worship, Bible study, or any other function or activity of the body of Christ.

ॐ Promise groups do not compete with or offer an alternative to any other group or organization, such as church, recovery, civic, charitable, political, leisure, or any other groups or organizations.

ॐ Because *The Promises* require humility, group participants should avoid projecting any false notion or impression of spiritual elitism.

ॐ No one should leave the meeting until it has been restored to its original or better condition.

Suggestions of decorum:

ॐ Immediately following the prayer and readings, each participant should introduce him or herself in turn in the following or equivalent manner: "Hi. My name is John Doe. I am *willing* to follow Jesus (or our Lord)."

ॐ This introduction should be repeated each time the person speaks during the meeting. This repeated practice is designed to reinforce humility. It eliminates cross-talk during sessions.

∾ Each meeting should conclude with participants forming a circle, holding hands, and reciting the Lord's Prayer, the Serenity Prayer, or some familiar benediction requiring the participation of all.

∾ Any dress is permissible if it is not provocative or indecent.

∾ **Participants in *The Promises* should be neither anonymous nor boastful. By all means, share your discovery, but in the context of offering the gospel of Jesus Christ to a fellow-sufferer.**

---

*A historical observation: Promise group meetings are patterned after Twelve Step meetings because of the latter's long history of proven effectiveness. Similarly, Twelve Step meetings derived many of their distinctive features from the Bible study discussion meetings of the Oxford Group. Thus, here is another example of how The Promises have helped to bring full circle the principles of holistic healing of Jesus Christ through the recovery movement back to their Christian origin.

About the Author

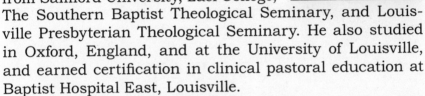

Glenn W. Nowell, Ph.D., D.Min., was ordained as a Southern Baptist minister on his twenty-first birthday in 1973 in Alabama where he held his first pastorate.

He graduated from Troy State University and earned graduate degrees from Samford University, Lael College, The Southern Baptist Theological Seminary, and Louisville Presbyterian Theological Seminary. He also studied in Oxford, England, and at the University of Louisville, and earned certification in clinical pastoral education at Baptist Hospital East, Louisville.

Dr. Nowell adopted Louisville, Kentucky, as his home before entering the United States Air Force as a chaplain and returned to Louisville upon his retirement from active duty in 1996.

As a chaplain, his reliance upon the Beatitudes, in the treatment of a variety of maladies, produced phenomenal success.

As a result, he became a sought-after advisor and referral of both federal and state mental health agencies. He discovered that his divinely-inspired methods worked when others failed.

Since his retirement, Dr. Nowell has devoted himself to a ministry of sharing biblical spirituality to treat individual, behavioral, and psychological disorders, dysfunctional families, and entire dysfunctional congregations caught in conflict.

Dr. Nowell is pastor of Hillview Baptist Church in Louisville where he enjoys unconditional joy with parishioners, has a radio ministry, and resides with wife Michaela and their son, Wes.